A JACOBITE ANTHOLOGY

The 1745 Association

*To commemorate the 250th Anniversary
of the Rising of 1745*

SCOTTISH CULTURAL PRESS

First published 1995
by
Scottish Cultural Press
PO Box 106
Aberdeen AB9 8ZE
Tel/Fax: 01224 583777

British Library Cataloguing in Publication Data
A catalogue record for this book is available from the British Library

ISBN 1 89821830 7

Typesetting by 'Fine Words!'
80 Woodlands Road
Lytham St. Annes
Lancashire FY8 1DA

Printed by Blackpool Printers Ltd.
5 - 7 Clare Street, Blackpool
Lancashire FY1 6HR

Prince Charles Edward Stuart
Artist unknown
(By courtesy of Barbara Fairweather)

FROM OUR PATRON

The Rt. Hon. the Earl of Perth

To celebrate widely an event of 250 years ago, when a Prince and seven followers landed in the far North of Scotland, is unusual. But the Prince was Bonnie Prince Charlie and, in the 18 months that followed, he and many of the Clans nearly changed British history. His was a romantic venture which has no parallel in Great Britain, unless it be the landing of William the Conqueror, who from the start had a strong Norman army with him.

James Francis Edward Stuart, his father, had landed 30 years before from France joining an army led, very badly, by Lord Mar - but the 'Fifteen' is another story more or less forgotten, whereas the 'Forty-Five' lives on, the subject of countless books, and more, surely, to come. The might of the British Navy and of the British Army with its Marlborough triumphs was arrayed against him, yet he nearly pulled it off. What if at Derby he had gone on towards a frightened London rather than retreated to Scotland?

For me, two facts stand out above all others during those 18 months: the paramount role of the Navy which prevented French money, arms and men coming to his help - though it failed to prevent his escape - and the almost irresistible force of the Highland Charge, such was the bravery of the Highlander. The search for Bonnie Prince Charlie after Culloden and his escape are the stuff of legend, of loyalty and of love, commemorated in song, in writing and the collecting of anything to do with him. On a personal note, in light of the active part my family, the Drummonds, took in the 'Forty-Five', I must plead guilty to being one of the collectors of all things Jacobite!

I write no more but rather draw attention to and praise the 50 years of the 1745 Association. Its 'Quarterly Notes' (now 'The Jacobite'), its gathering of new facts and its promoting by monuments the great events of that time are splendid work. All who care should join the Association and take part in its activities.

Sir Donald Cameron of Lochiel, K.T., C.V.O.

The year 1995 is a very important year for the 1745 Association, for not only will it commemorate the 250th anniversary of the Raising of the Standard at Glenfinnan on 19 August 1745 but it also marks the 50th year of the 1745 Association.

As Patron of this Association, it gives me great pleasure to write a brief foreward to this anthology of articles from "The Jacobite" and to congratulate the Association on their work and activities during the past 50 years.

I have, for many years, enjoyed reading the articles in "The Jacobite" which are nearly always well-researched, well-written and of great interest to all students of Jacobite history. To pick out just a few of these articles for inclusion in this anthology must have been a difficult task, but it is certainly right to record the recent dedication in the Savoy Chapel of the plaque in memory of Dr. Archie Cameron of Lochiel, and also, of course, the erection of the cairn at Loch nan Uamh which is such a fine memorial to Prince Charles Edward, and reflects great credit on the '45 Association who were largely responsible for it.

The anniversary of the Raising of the Standard at Glenfinnan this year will be a memorable event and naturally of great interest to members of the 1745 Association.

I remember that, in 1945 when they were celebrating the 200th anniversary, my father, who was one of the speakers on that occasion, was careful to point out "that Highlanders of today were faithful subjects to their present Majesty, King George VI," but to balance this with the fact that "their forebears had been just as loyal to the man whom they considered was their lawful Sovereign." These sentiments of loyalty to our Sovereign, together with fond memories of 1745 and the start of Prince Charles Edward's adventure, are held as strongly today as they were on that occasion fifty years ago.

I commend the initiative of the Association in putting together this anthology of old "Jacobite" articles which many readers will recollect and read again with great pleasure. It is a most appropriate way to mark the 50th year of the Association, and I hope it meets with the acclaim it deserves.

Donald Cameron of Lochiel

FROM THE EDITOR

1995-96 marks the 250th anniversary of the 1745 Jacobite Rising, the time, often called "The Year of the Prince", from June 1745 when Prince Charles Edward Stuart landed in the Western Isles to September 1746 when he and his followers left Loch nan Uamh for France.

1995-96 is also the 50th anniversary of the 1745 Association, formed shortly after the National Trust's commemorative ceremony at Glenfinnan in 1945 to mark the 200th anniversary of the Raising of the Standard. One of the founder members was Marion Cameron, our Secretary for many years and a devoted Jacobite, to whom I am greatly indebted for much information about the Association and for my own enthusiasm for the '45. Our aims were then, and still are, to keep green the memory of the brave men and women of the '45, to mark sites of Jacobite interest, and to further an enlightened study of the history of the House of Stuart and the Jacobite period.

In 1956, our steadfast members Seton Gordon and Francis Cameron-Head of Inverailort, having learned from local oral tradition the site of the Prince's escape to France, proposed that the Association raise a commemorative cairn at Loch nan Uamh. This was duly done. Since then, we have placed cairns at Kinlochmoidart, in memory of the seven companions who landed with the Prince from France, and at High Bridge, to commemorate the first skirmish of the campaign. Memorial plaques have been dedicated at Dalilea House to the Bard of Clanranald, at Cille Choirill to Keppoch and Tirnadris and at the Queen's Chapel of the Savoy in London to Dr. Archibald Cameron. We have contributed to the upkeep of the memorial to the Battle of Falkirk and of the grave of Flora MacDonald at Kilmuir and have recently taken over responsibility for the grave of Roderick MacKenzie in Glenmoriston.

We are honoured to count among our members not only our present patrons but also such illustrious names as the Countess of Erroll, Hereditary Lord High Constable of Scotland, Sir Iain Moncrieffe of that Ilk, Sir Robert Menzies, Prime Minister of Australia, Sir Compton Mackenzie, and Lord Lurgan who generously gifted to the Association our oil painting of the Raising of the Standard at Glenfinnan, now housed in Glenfinnan House Hotel.

Since fairly early in its history, the Association's annual meetings have expanded into the Annual Gatherings we still enjoy now, when members from far and near meet at some centre with Jacobite connections for a three-day programme of visits and social events. Recent Gatherings have been in Aberdeen, Stirling, Penrith and Skye.

Our membership is worldwide and includes not only those whose ancestors were supporters of the Stuarts but anyone who has a genuine interest in Jacobite history. It was with grateful thanks that we obtained financial backing from the Glencoe Foundation Inc., Delaware, USA that helped us to realise a long-held ambition to publish "The Muster Roll of Prince Charles Edward Stuart's Army". Dr. MacKie's "Prince's Army List" came into the possession of the Association in the 1950's but it was not until 1984 that we were able to finance its publication. Much credit is due to the three joint editors, Alastair Livingstone of Bachuil, Christian Aikman and Betty Stuart Hart, who gallantly undertook this formidable task. The book was very well received and a great deal more information about the Prince's army has come to light as a result of its publication.

An important part of the work of the Association has been the production of a regular periodical for members, until quite recently known as "The Quarterly Notes" and now called "The Jacobite" and for many years edited by Barbara Fairweather of Glencoe. Many members, as well as Council members and speakers at our Annual Gatherings, have contributed to these journals over the years, and it is from these articles that we have compiled this small book. It has not been possible to include everyone just as it has not been possible to include all facets of the '45. We hope, however, that by bringing together some of the people and events, both well-known and little-known, we have marked fittingly the anniversary of the Rising of 1745.

The cover design of a Jacobite Rose is by Edgar Wyard, a former Vice-Chairman of the 1745 Association, who also created our motif on the title page. The fine drawings of the cairns at Kinlochmoidart and at Highbridge, and of the glass, the pistol, the targe and broadswords, etc., are by Sharon Butterfield, and those of Dalilea House and of the ship are by the Rev. James Duffy.

My personal thanks are due to all those friends in the Association who have helped to produce this book.

Anne Scholey

CONTENTS

Prince Charles Edward's silver travelling canteen, made for him in 1740
by Ebenezer Oliphant, the Edinburgh silversmith.
(Courtesy of the National Museums of Scotland)

ITINERARY OF PRINCE CHARLES EDWARD
*The dates are Old Style

1745

July 23: Landed on Eriskay, Outer Hebrides

July 25: Sailed to Loch nan Uamh - landed at Borrodale, near the house of Angus MacDonald. Spent the time in correspondence, sending messengers to the chiefs and others.

Aug 11: By sea to Kinlochmoidart House - joined by John Murray of Broughton

Aug 18: Marched to Loch Shiel - sailed to Glenaladale

Aug 19: Arrived at Glenfinnan where the Standard was raised

Aug 21: Left Glenfinnan

Aug 28: Marched over the Corrieyairack Pass

Aug 31: Arrived at Blair Castle in Atholl

Sept 4: Arrived at Perth and remained until 10th - joined by many leading Jacobite gentry

Sept 14: Marched round Stirling to Falkirk

Sept 17: Entered Edinburgh and stayed at Holyrood - the army camped at Duddingston

Sept 21: Battle of Prestonpans (Gladsmuir)

Sept 22: The Prince stayed at Holyrood until October 31st - a great many Jacobites joined him

Nov 1: Marched to Dalkeith and through the Borders

Nov 8: Crossed the River Esk into England

Nov 10: Reached Carlisle - the siege lasted until 14th

Nov 30: Reached Manchester - a considerable number joined and formed the Manchester Regiment, under the command of Francis Townley

Dec 4: The Prince entered Derby and lodged in the house of Lord Exeter

Dec 6: Black Friday - the retreat began

Dec 18: Skirmish at Clifton - Lord George Murray's force beat off an attack by Cumberland's cavalry

Dec 19: The Prince reached Carlisle - garrison left, including the Manchester Regiment

Dec 20: Marched north to Glasgow by Dumfries and Nithsdale

Dec 26: Entered Glasgow - stayed until Jan 3rd. Whole army reviewed

1746

Jan 4: Marched towards Stirling, where the Prince made his HQ at Bannockburn House - stayed until 31st.

Jan 17: Battle of Falkirk

Feb 1: Withdrawal began - the Army crossed the Forth and the Prince lodged at Drummond Castle

Feb 6-9:	At Blair Castle
Feb 16:	At Moy Hall - guest of Lady MacIntosh - the Rout of Moy
Feb 19:	At Culloden House
Feb 20:	Inverness Castle surrendered
Mar 3-10:	At Inverness - stayed in the house of the Dowager Lady MacIntosh
Mar 11-20:	Travelled to Elgin - visited Gordon Castle - became ill. Jacobite forces besieged Fort Augustus and Fort William and were active north of Inverness. Lord George Murray blockaded Blair Castle.
Mar 21-31:	The Prince returned to Inverness - Lord John Drummond in charge of defence of the Spey - HQ at Gordon Castle
Apr 1-13:	The Duke of Perth and Lord John Drummond retired before Cumberland's advance by Forres and Nairn to Culloden
Apr 14:	The Prince at Culloden House
Apr 15:	March by night to Nairn to surprise Cumberland - obliged to abandon the attack
Apr 16:	Marched back in the morning to Drumossie Moor - Battle of Culloden - after the battle, the Prince crossed the River Nairn at the ford of Faillie, where he dismissed his cavalry escort, and rode off to Stratherrick and Gortleg, where he met Lord Lovat.
Apr 17:	Arrived early morning at Invergarry Castle - then continued to Glen Pean via Loch Arkaig
Apr 20:	Reached Borrodale on foot
Apr 26:	Sailed from Borrodale to the Outer Hebrides - landed in Benbecula
Ap 27-Jul 27	Wanderings in the Outer Isles
June 28:	Sailed to Skye dressed as "Betty Burke" in the company of Flora MacDonald
June 29:	Landed near Monkstat House in the north of Skye - spent the night at Kingsburgh House.
July 5:	Returned to the mainland - landed at Mallaig
July 10-13:	Sheltered in a cave at Borrodale
July 13-23:	Wanderings in Moidart and Knoydart
July 24-28:	Joined by the Eight Men of Glenmoriston in the cave at Corrie a gho
Aug 28-Sept 13:	Wanderings in Badenoch - hiding in Cluny's Cage on Ben Alder.
Sept 13:	Travelled west to Loch nan Uamh
Sept 19:	Went on board the French ship "L'Heureux"
Sept 20:	Sailed for France

Note: Great Britain retained the Old Style Julian calendar until 1752 while Roman Catholic countries in Europe adopted the New Style Gregorian system, leaving British dates 10 days behind.

C.W.H.A.

THE SEVEN MEN OF MOIDART

by N. H. MacDonald

The original row of seven beech trees in the field adjacent to the road from Acharacle to Glenuig, representing the seven followers who landed at Borradale on 25 July, 1745, with Prince Charles Edward Stuart and which have become known as "The Seven men of Moidart", were planted about 1820 by authority of the then proprietors of the Kinlochmoidart Estate, Margarita, heiress of the last MacDonald laird of Kinlochmoidart and her husband, Lieut-Colonel David Robertson who, after his marriage adopted the surname of Robertson-MacDonald. The Seven Men of Moidart were William Murray, Marquis of Tullibardine, regarded by the Jacobites as the 2nd Duke of Atholl; Sir Thomas Sheridan, an Irishman who had been the Prince's preceptor; Sir John MacDonald, or MacDonnell, an Irish cavalry officer in the French army; Aeneas MacDonald, a Paris banker and younger brother of the Laird of Kinlochmoidart; John William O'Sullivan, an Irish officer in the French army; the Rev. George Kelly, an Irish Protestant clergyman in the Prince's service, and Francis Strickland, an English gentleman from Westmorland. Of these, Tullibardine died in captivity, Sheridan, O'Sullivan and Kelly escaped to France, Aeneas MacDonald was banished, Sir John MacDonald surrendered as a prisoner of war and Francis Strickland died at Carlisle.

3

The sea-bindweed or convolvulus (Calystegia soldanella) is closely associated with Prince Charles Edward. Before embarking for Scotland, the Prince walked along the French shore and gathered some of the seeds of this plant. When he first set foot on Scottish soil, on the island of Eriskay, he scattered the seeds which grew and seeded. To this day the flower appears but does not grow on other Hebridean islands. It is sometimes called the Prince's flower.

Barbara Fairweather

KINLOCHMOIDART

Here, in your steps I follow,
Prince of a thousand hearts,
Who came as the Summer swallow
Comes, and departs.

Brief was your stay and arid;
Sad as the curlew's cry,
Wandering hunted, harried,
Under God's sky.

Though but a dream uncaptured,
Still to your tale forlorn,
There shall listen, enraptured,
Children unborn.

M.D. Cameron of Clunes

4

ALASDAIR MACMHAIGHSTIR ALASDAIR
THE JACOBITE BARD OF CLANRANALD

by Norman H. MacDonald

Alexander MacDonald, or Alasdair MacMhaighstir Alasdair (Alexander the son of Master Alexander) as he is better known to the Gael, the most prominent bard of the Forty-Five, indeed of Gaeldom prior to and after that great event, was born about 1700 in the Parish of Island Finnan, probably at Dalilea, the residence of his father, the Rev. Alexander MacDonald, Minister of Island Finnan - Maighstir (Master Alexander) to his parishioners.

Little is known of the bard's early life. He probably received his elementary education from his father, a graduate of Glasgow and no mean scholar. Young Alasdair, it is said, while yet a child "lisped in numbers" and began to rhyme early, his first act in this direction being to satirise his own father.

He was apparently sent to the University of Glasgow at an early age but of his scholastic attainments at that institution there is no record other than that he was well educated and a good Classical scholar. He appears to have left the university prematurely and to have married, while young, Janet MacDonald, a native of Glencoe, by whom he had one son and four daughters.

In 1729, Alasdair was appointed teacher of a charity school at Island Finnan, by the Society for Propagating Christian Knowledge (SPCK), but the Society were not entirely satisfied with his behaviour and admonished him for neglecting his duties in 1735.

In 1741 he published his Gaelic-English Vocabulary, a volume of 200 pages and the first Scottish Gaelic vocabulary ever to be published. In the summer of 1744 he was unaccountably absent from home and his son, Ranald, was acting as substitute at the school. The Minister of Ardnamurchan reported on 15 July 1745: "that the Charity School has been vacant from Whitsunday last by the voluntary desertion of Alexander macDonald, the former schoolmaster". No fault was found with his professional efficiency but he was accused of composing and singing indecent songs and subsequently dismissed from his post. Alasdair, however, had by that time found new interests and it is probable that his conversion to Roman Catholicism took place about this time. A popular anecdote concerning him relates that the morning after a heavy drinking bout, a colleague asked him how he felt and the latter retorted that he had been in Hell. "Did you get burnt by the fire, Alasdair?" "No" replied the Bard, "I could not get near it for ministers!"

Alasdair could hardly have been unaware of the probable landing of the Prince which had been generally anticipated after the defeat of the British under the Duke of Cumberland by the French at Fontenoy on 11 May 1745, and when the "Du Tellay" brought Charles from Eriskay to Arisaig, Alasdair hastened to welcome his royal kinsman at Loch nan Uamh. When they met, the Bard did not recognise the Prince on account of his disguise and proceeded to make free with him until a warning glance from a fellow clansman made him realise that the person with whom he was speaking was of high station.

He received the first commission in the Prince's Army, that of a captaincy in the Clanranald Regiment, being in command of 50 "cliver fellows" raised by him in Ardnamurchan, and was appointed to teach the Prince Gaelic due to his "skill in the Highland language". His songs: 'Oran Nuadh' - 'A New Song', 'Oran Fineachan Gaidhealach' - 'The Song of the Highland Clans', and 'Oran do'n Phrionnsa' - 'A Song to the Prince', show clearly the enthusiasm with which the Prince's arrival was awaited by the Highland Jacobites and in particular the Bard himself. These poems were sent to Aeneas MacDonald, the banker, Kinlochmoidart's brother in Paris, who read them in English to the Prince thus encouraging him to come to Scotland. Alasdair, therefore, may well have indirectly contributed a great deal to starting the Forty-Five. He was one of the first to arrive at Glenfinnan for the historic raising of the Standard, on 19 August, which signalled the commencement of the Prince's campaign, when the Bard is said to have sung his song of welcome: 'Tearlach Mac Sheumais' - 'Charles, Son of James'.

He served throughout the campaign until the defeat at Culloden, after which he and his eldest brother, Angus, 2nd of Dalilea, found shelter for a short time among the woods and caves of their own neighbourhood. Eventually, the search for the Prince became so intense that it became necessary for him to take his wife and family to the hills, his house and effects being plundered by the Hanoverians, even his cat being killed lest it might provide sustenance for his wife and children. During their wanderings, his wife gave birth to a daughter and they finally found shelter with her relatives in Glencoe, where they remained until the Act of Indemnity was passed in 1747.

On 28 December 1747, he brought Bishop Forbes, author of the "Lyon in Mourning", in Leith, an account of the Prince's wandering after Culloden, prepared jointly by himself, Young Clanranald, and MacDonald of Glenaladale. The account suggests that Alasdair accompanied the Prince for at least part of the time. The Bishop writes of Alasdair: "He is a very smart, acute man, remarkably well skilled in the Erse, for he can both read and write Irish language in its original character, a piece of knowledge almost lost in the Highlands of Scotland, there being exceedingly few that have any skill at all that way. For the Captain (the Bishop always referred to Alasdair in such a manner) told me that he did not know another person (old Clanranald excepted) that knew anything of the first tongue in its original character . . ."

6

In 1751 he visited Edinburgh for the purpose of publishing a volume of poems. "It is" as has been said, "very characteristic of his reckless courage that he published these poems, breathing rebellion in every line, and pouring the vails of his wrath upon the whole race of the Georges, five years after the battle of Culloden." The unsold copies in the hands of the publisher were seized and burnt at the Cross in Edinburgh by the common hangman. Alasdair expected but escaped prosecution, settling finally in Arisaig.

His last moments are described in Father Charles MacDonald's "Moidart; or Among the Clanranalds" as follows: "In his last illness he was carefully nursed by his Arisaig friends, two of whom on the night of his decease, finding the hours rather monotonous, and thinking he was asleep, began to recite in an undertone some verses of their own composition. To their astonishment however, the bard raised himself up, and, smiling at their inexperienced efforts, pointed out how the ideas might be improved and the verses made to run in another and smoother form at the same time giving an illustration in a few original measures of his own. He than sank back on the pillow and immediately expired. it was proposed at first to carry his remains to Eilean Fhionnain - Island Finnan - but the project, owing to a severe gale then raging along the coast, had to be abandoned. The Arisaig people thereupon got their own way and Alasdair MacMhaighstir Alasdair was buried in the cemetery of Kilmorie, close to the present Catholic Church of Arisaig."

Dalilea House

THE SKIRMISH OF HIGHBRIDGE

By Norman H MacDonald

About the 2nd of August, 1745, the authorities in Edinburgh were informed that Prince Charles Edward had landed in the West Highlands and Lieutenant-General Sir John Cope, Commander-in-Chief of the forces in Scotland immediately began to make preparations to march north to quell the expected insurrection.

On the 11th of August, Cope received a communication from the Deputy Governor of Fort William claiming "that 2000 French were landed in Moydart". The General then sent Campbell of Inverawe's Company by way of Argyll to Fort William and "a thousand stand of arms" to Inverness. He sent further orders to two companies of the Royal Scots, recently raised at Perth, and for Captain Sweetenham, Commandant at Ruthven Barracks, considered a good engineer, also to make haste for Fort William, the latter with orders to take command of the garrison there.

Donald MacDonell of Lochgarry, Glengarry's cousin german, having heard rumours of the proposed reinforcement of Fort William, lay in ambush with a body of Glengarry's men at the head of the Corrieyairack Pass and observing Captain Sweetenham with his servants and baggage approaching, detached four of his men to apprehend them. Sweetenham was subsequently handed over by Lochgarry to John Gordon of Glenbucket, Glengarry's father-in-law, who carried him to the Prince who later released him on parole.

Meanwhile, the two companies of the Royal Scots, commanded by Captain John Scott, son of Scotstarvit and later to become General Scott of Balcomie, were on the morning of the 16th August, on the military road between Fort Augustus and Fort William. Scott and his detachment had passed Lochs Oich and Lochy without incident and began descending by the road, which can still be traced in the field behind the present Kilmonivaig Church building, towards the steep narrow bridge across the river Spean known as Highbridge, about nine miles from Fort William, which is surrounded by boulders and thick woods.

Keppoch had received intelligence of the approach of this force, about 80 or 90 strong, the commanding officer of which had apparently sent out no scouts or advance party, with only about two hours to spare and although he had then only a few men assembled, resolved to prevent them from reaching their destination. To endeavour by strategem what he could not accomplish by force, Keppoch sent his cousin german, Donald MacDonell of Tirnadris with eleven men and a piper to a little inn at Highbridge, to await the arrival of the enemy until he could gather a sufficient body of his Clan to engage them.

Tirnadris, in order to make the best use of the small force under his command, placed them behind the inn commanding the bridge over the Spean. When Scott's force appeared on the opposite bank above the bridge, Tirnadris ordered the piper to play and rushed out from behind the building "with a loud huzza", while his men followed his example and darted about among the neighbouring trees and undergrowth. Scott immediately halted his men who were struck with terror, and sent forward his servant and a sergeant to discover the strength of the Highlanders. The men were allowed to cross the bridge after which two of Tirnadris' men sprang out from the woods and dragged them off as prisoners.

This incident was more than enough for the already panic-stricken soldiers and although Captain Scott himself was in favour of attempting to continue his route, his fellow officers, Captain James Thomson and Lieutenants Rose and Fergusson, pleaded with him, on account of the low morale of their men, to abandon the attempt. Scott eventually yielded to their remonstrances and ordered a retreat which soon developed into a disorderly rabble. The Highlanders, allowing them to get some distance away before taking up the pursuit, followed cautiously, Tirnadris being careful not to reveal the smallness of their number.

While the disorderly retreat of the redcoats continued, the MacDonells were joined, at Lowbridge, by some of the Dochanasie Camerons and more of their own clansmen. After pursuing the soldiers for five or six miles, the Highlanders, though still very much outnumbered, considered themselves strong enough to come up with the enemy and began firing. The redcoats, whom Scott had by now managed to form into a hollow square, continued their retreat, firing indiscriminately at Tirnadris and his men as they went, until all their ammunition was exhausted, without having inflicted a single casualty among the Highlanders, who by this time, with the arrival of Keppoch, had increased to around 45 or 50 at most, not half of whom were armed. The regulars, in their panic, began to break ranks and run. Scott and his brother officers did all they could to prevent their force from disintegrating and managed to restore some order but they were finally brought to a halt at Laggan Achadrom, near the northern end of Loch Lochy, where they found their way blocked by about 50 of Glengarry's men.

The Highlanders poured several volleys into the disorganised force by which Captain Scott was wounded in the shoulder, a sergeant and 3 or 4 other ranks killed and about a dozen wounded. All organised resistance now having ceased, Keppoch with drawn sword, advanced quickly and alone towards the soldiers and warned that if they did not immediately lay down their arms and surrender, they would all be cut to pieces. Scott, aware that Keppoch was making no idle threat, immediately acquiesced.

9

Soon after the surrender, Lochiel, to whom Keppoch had sent a message informing him of the affair, arrived with a few men on the other side of Loch Lochy. About 7 pm the prisoners were conveyed to an inn at Achnacarry and Captain Scott was carried to Lochiel's residence where he was treated like a guest. Lochiel sent word to Fort William informing the Governor of Captain Scott's condition and requesting that a surgeon be sent from the fort to dress his wounds. This request was refused.

The prisoners were later marched unarmed in a body to the Prince at Glenfinnan, flanked on either side by a division of the Clan Cameron with Lochiel at their head, to attend the ceremony of unfurling the Royal Standard of King James VIII, on the 19th of August. Keppoch arrived later with 300 men. Captain Scott and his fellow officers were eventually released by the Prince on parole.

Thus ended the first military engagement of the Forty-five which served to boost the morale of the Jacobites and the aspirations of the Prince.

The Glenfinnan Monument with the symbolic roses of James VIII,
Charles Edward and Henry Benedict *(Drawing by Edgar Wyard)*

GLENFINNAN

A great quiet now has settled in the glen,
    And Prince Charlie stands for ever watching for the men
To march with him again, Alas! to march with him again.
    They gathered here in '45, the Clans of the Old Gael;
They gathered and went forth to battle, and the tale -
    Half forgotten, half remembered - is ended in the wail
O' the winds across deserted crofts along Glenaladale.
    For the men of Moidart, Ailort, of Lochiel and Borrodale
Have wandered forth across the seas with unreturning sail.
    A great quiet now has settled on the Glen
And Prince Charlie stands forever waiting for the men
    To march with him again, Alas! to march with him again.

Patrick J Little

The standard raised at Glenfinnan on August 19th, 1745, was of red and
white silk and was sewn by the ladies of Kinlochmoidart House.

Prince Charles Edward stayed at Fassifern after the Raising of the
Standard. Here, it is said, he leaned out of his bedroom window and plucked a
white rose (of rosa alba maxima) which grows up the wall. He is also said to have
plucked a white rose at Ardblair from a plant of rosa semi-plena.

Barbara Fairweather

11

ROUTE OF PRINCE CHARLIE'S ARMY FROM FASSIFERN TO MOY

By Donald B. MacCulloch

One point of dispute in the outward march of Prince Charlie and his army is the route which they followed from Fassifern to Moy. Drummond Norie, the well known writer on the 'Forty-Five' campaign, says in his "*Life and Adventures of Prince Charles Edward Stuart*". Vol. 1, page 202, that when the Prince and his army left Fassifern they proceeded up Glen Suileag and through Glen Loy to Moy. In my book "*Romantic Lochaber*" I think I have given sufficiently convincing evidence to disprove this opinion. My evidence leads me to believe that when they left Fassifern they proceeded along the road, or track by the north shore of Loch Eil, then up the course of the Annat Burn (on the Ordnance Survey maps it is named Allt Dogha) and through Glen Laragain, sometimes called Glen Sheangain; thence to Moy. Lack of space in "*Romantic Lochaber*" prevented me from giving the following local tradition in support of the route I believe Prince Charlie and his army to have followed from Fassifern to Moy. I learned this tradition during my youth when in my home-village of Corpach which adjoins Annat and is about five miles from Fassifern.

At that time the proprietor of Corpach Hotel was a gentleman named Colin MacPherson who was well versed in local lore and a fluent Gaelic speaker. Mr MacPherson told my father that at the end of last century there were an old man and wife living in a little thatched cottage at Annat, where their ancestors had lived for generations. This cottage stood on the outer side of the west boundary wall of Annat Farm and quite close to the main road. When I first knew that cottage the walls were still standing but the thatch roof had disintegrated, though some of the rough wooden 'cabars', or roof struts, lay scattered within. The low crumbling walls were demolished and the stones used for a naval building erected nearby during the Second World War.

Mr MacPherson had been very friendly with that old couple (he had really been very good to them). He said they had an old wooden armchair which they prized very much and in which no one but special friends was allowed to sit. A piece of string tied and stretched from arm to arm prevented others from sitting on it. They told Mr MacPherson that their fondness for that chair was because Prince Charlie had sat on it.

This is the story which they told about the chair. When Prince Charlie and his army left Fassifern they marched along the road, or track, by the shore of Loch Eil until they reached the Annat Burn. Here they halted. Then three officers crossed the stepping stones in the burn and walked over to the cottage. The couple who lived in the cottage at that time were up in years but quite active. The wife was standing at the door when the officers came forward and she recognised one

12

of them as Lochiel but did not know the other two. Lochiel asked if they could have a talk with her husband. She invited the three of them into the cottage and told them to sit down while she fetched her husband who was doing some work at the back of the cottage. When she and her husband entered they saw one of the officers sitting in their wooden armchair but Lochiel and the other officer were standing. Lochiel said to her husband that he wanted someone who was well acquainted with the banks of the Annat Burn and Glen Laragain to guide the army over this route because they had some guns to drag and they wished to avoid all bogs and soft ground. The husband said "My son is in your army but he does not know this route as well as I do so I will guide you myself. I know every inch of the ground." Lochiel thanked him and, turning towards the officer seated in the chair, said, "This is your Prince." The Prince rose to his feet and shook hands with the couple and then went out of the cottage with Lochiel and the other officer and signalled to the army to advance up the west bank of the Annat Burn.

After guiding the army and guns safely to the main road, or track, at Sheangain, the husband was thanked by the Prince who gave him some money. From that time onward the old wooden armchair was preserved carefully through each generation. When the old man whom Mr MacPherson knew died his wife gave the old wooden armchair to Mr MacPherson as a present for his kindness to them. In later years I saw that old chair when Mr MacPherson lived in retirement in "Dal-na-Rois" at Corpach.

THE CORRIEYAIRACK PASS

Two hundred years ago George Wade
For war built bridge and highway.
Now commerce finer roads has made,
But I'll keep Wade's for my way.
For when you and I went wandering
We knew all tumult cease;
And birds and beasts had mind of us,
And suns and stars were kind for us,
And we were glad to find for us
Wade's quiet ways of peace.

These lines (from *Wade in Scotland* by J. B. Salmond) tell, with admirable brevity, the story of the military roads constucted in the eighteenth century by General Wade of Scotland. Of these, the Corrieyairack Pass, climbing the slopes from Fort Augustus to Laggan, is the most spectacular. The Jacobite forces availed themselves of it in 1745 and it was used by drovers and travellers until, about a hundred years later, it was superseded by less formidable routes. The passage of time and the elements have caused some destruction but the challenge of its traverses, its solitude and its wide prospects have continued to give pleasure to walkers and lovers of nature.

C.W.H.A.

LADY LUDE

By J Barrie Robertson

En route from Old Blair to Blair Atholl village we had a glimpse of Lude House, situated at some distance away. The Robertsons of Lude were, like the majority of Clan Donnachaidh, loyal and devoted adherents of the Stuarts and they greatly influenced the Athollmen to rally to the banner of the Marquis of Montrose, which was raised on the estate of Lude. Eventually the mansion of Lude was burned by the troops of Cromwell, who exacted a fine from its owner. Prince Charles honoured Lude with a visit in 1745 on the march southward. Some historians state that on each of the three nights the Prince stayed at Blair Atholl he slept at Blair Castle, others say that he stayed over one night at Lude. What is certain is that he attended a Highland Ball at Lude. Members will recall seeing at our ceilidh in Pitlochry a fine red Robertson tartan jacket said to have been worn by the Prince at this ball. The widowed Lady Lude, who was a cousin of the Jacobite Duke William of Atholl and acted as hostess to the Prince at Blair Castle, had her own company in the Atholl Brigade of the army. She threatened that if any deserters should return to the district she would have them hanged from her gate-posts. Lady Lude was made a prisoner in 1746.

14

CRIEFF IN THE '45

By M. G. Selkirk

Today, Crieff is principally a holiday resort set on a sunny slope on the southern flanks of the Grampian Mountains in Perthshire. In 1745, however, the town manufactured shoes, linen and cloth. Here, too, was held an annual Tryst, or Cattle Market, when herds from all over the Highlands and Islands were driven to the sales to be bought by Lowland and English cattle dealers. From its lofty position, Crieff looks down on the broad agricultural valley of Strathearn, fertile and productive.

When the news of the raising of the Prince's Standard at Glenfinnan reached the town, it generated mixed emotions. The inhabitants of Crieff were not especially drawn to the Jacobite cause, despite the fact that only a couple of miles south stands Drummond Castle, in 1745 the home of James Drummond, 3rd Duke of Perth. The Duke, a stalwart supporter of the Prince, was also the owner of a large proportion of the land on which Crieff stands. He and his family had brought industries to the town and generally improved the lot of the people, but memories were long. It was recalled that in January 1716, following the inconclusive Battle of Sheriffmuir, most of Crieff had been burnt down on the instructions of the Earl of Mar. All houses and crops were destroyed throughout Strathearn to deny shelter and forage to the Duke of Argyll's troops who were following close behind the Highland army. Being left homeless on a cold winter's night did not endear the townsfolk to another uprising for the same purpose.

There were exceptions, of course. Apart from the Duke of Perth, who raised a regiment for the Prince, comprised in part of his estate workers and dependants, a small number of sympathisers in the town declared for the Jacobite cause and followed the Prince on his quest.

Crieff's somewhat unwilling appearance in the limelight of the Uprising began with a two day spell, from the 20th to the 22nd August 1745, when General Sir John Cope came rattling up the military road from Stirling with whatever troops he could muster, to try to head off the Jacobite army, newly raised at Glenfinnan. He encamped on what is now an 18-hole golf course on the east side of the town. A well there, from which his troops drew water, is still known as Cope's Well. Life in the town then returned to normal, even to the extent of holding the annual Cattle Tryst that October as usual. Drovers and buyers alike were given safe passage by both sides. The south needed beef and the Highlands needed the money.

GRAY'S MILL

By George Gibb

At Gray's Mill - so called, it is believed, after some early miller of note who has left only his name - situated a little to the north of the village of Slateford is a small room, still inhabited, in which Prince Charlie resided for a short time in September, 1745. Here his deputies from the city made rendezvous with the Prince in the negotiations to arrange for the capitulation of the City of Edinburgh-protracted proceedings which were suddenly ended by the entry of 900 Highlanders into the Capital headed by Cameron of Lochiel.

The little window above the doorway is said to be the room in which the Prince slept, and through which he must have watched the clansmen encamped in front. The iron ring to which his steed was secured upon his arrival still keeps its hold to one of the stable lintels of the farm.

I regret to say that the farm and farmer's house were demolished about ten years ago. However, the old pantiles of the roof have been used again on the present building which belongs to Macnab of the Scottish Dyers.

The new bridge, built about 1937, which carries the Union Canal over the Lanark road, commemorates the fact that near this spot Prince Charlie's armies camped at Gray's Mill before the occupation of the City of Edinburgh.

SONG

By Cornet William Home

(Cornet William Home wrote the following poem soon after the Battle of Prestonpans, at which he was present. He was fourteen years old.)

> To arms! to arms! my bonny Highland laddie
> To arms! to arms at the beat of the drum
> The French horn sounded, put on your kilts and plaidies
> For CHARLEY the Prince Regent is come.
> There's never a Clan that trips over the plain
> But must buckle to the Man that is five foot ten
> And the tune they strike to the tabor and pipe
> Is the King shall enjoy his own again.
>
> At Prestonpans a very pleasant story
> A smarter engagement ne'er yet was seen
> The Red Coated band instead of winning glory
> Fled, while the blood ran o'er the plain
> While cowardly Cope being destitute of hope
> Did suddenly elope, and forsook his men
> To fly he must, he thought it but just
> That the King should enjoy his own again.

16

A PROPOSED JACOBITE COINAGE FOR 1745

by Michael Sharp

It is well know that James VIII issued warrants to Norbert Roettier, his Engraver General, to prepare puncheons and dies for striking coinages in 1708 and 1716. One English crown dated 1709 is known to have been struck and dies for Scottish guineas and crowns dated 1716 were made. These dies were acquired by Matthew Young, a numismatist, in 1828. From those dies, by then a little rusty, he produced a limited number of specimens in various metals. Original strikings are unknown.

It is also known that Robert Strange, who was present at Prestonpans, Falkirk and Culloden, was commissioned by Charles, Prince Regent, shortly before that last fateful battle to produce plates for printing paper money. A plate for one, two, three and six penny notes was found after the battle and handed to Cluny MacPherson; it can now be seen in the West Highland Museum, Fort William. Since Prince Charles had, in modern parlance, slipped away to 'go it alone' it is not surprising that no warrant was issued by his father for a coinage.

Study of the Atholl Papers, however, reveals that one was contemplated as a letter, reproduced below, from Lieutenant-General Lord George Murray written in Edinburgh, where he was recruiting after the success at Prestonpans, to his eldest brother William, Marquis of Tullibardine and de-jure Duke of Atholl, shows. This is the only reference to a Jacobite coinage for the '45 I have encountered. It is unfortunate that there is no reference to the engraver and die-sinker: Robert Strange might enter one's considerations.

Dear Brother,

I received your letter of the 29 September . . . I have been pressing about money to be sent to you, both formerly and now, as if my life depended on it. There is £300 sent at present, mostly in specie.

It is proposed to get in all the plate we can and coin shillings for, besides the want of cash in general, there is great penury of silver. The town of Glasgow have given £5,500 in bank notes, bills on London and some merchandise. For God's sake send up what men of your own people you can and don't let them wait for anybody else; and his Royal Highness desires, as soon as the Frasers, MacIntoshes and McPhersons come up, that you would also yourself come in person.

The castle of Edinburgh fired a good deal last evening . . . The money sent you just now is £100 in bank notes, £100 in Louis d'ors and £100 in guineas. I would gladly have got £500 but it was not possible.

I am, your faithful, humble servant,

George Murray, Wednesday, 10 in the morning.

A TALE OF A WHITE COCKADE

By Donald J. Macdonald of Castleton

When the Prince's Army took Carlisle on their way south, a party of the Clan Donald was sent out foraging in the country around. It was commanded by a Captain MacDonald, who was probably Ranald Og of Kinlochmoidart. They approached Rose Castle and the following letter from Lady Clerk of Penicuik tells what happened:

To Blackwood's Magazine, Edinburgh, 21st April, 1817

Sir,

According to your request this morning, I send you some account of the particulars that attended my birth, which I do with infinite pleasure as it reflects great honour on the Highlanders to whom I always feel the greatest gratitude that, at a time when their hearts were set on plunder, the fear of hurting a sick lady and her child stopped their intentions!

This incident occurred on November 15th, 1745. My father, Mr. D'Acre, then an officer in His Majesty's militia, was a prisoner in the Castle of Carlisle, at that time in the hands of Prince Charles. My mother (daughter of Sir George Fleming, Bart., Bishop of Carlisle) was living at Rose Castle, six miles from Carlisle, where she was delivered of me. She had given orders that I should immediately be baptised by the Bishop's chaplain (his lordship not being at home) by the names of Rosemary D'Acre. At that moment a company of Highlanders appeared, headed by a Captain MacDonald; who, having heard there was much plate and valuables in the Castle, came to plunder it. Upon the approach of the Highlanders an old gray-haired servant ran out and entreated Captain MacDonald not to proceed as any noise or alarm might occasion the death of both lady and child. The Captain enquired when the lady had been confined. "Within the hour", the servant replied. MacDonald stopped. The servant added: "They are just going to christen the infant." MacDonald, taking off his cockade said, "Let her be christened with this cockade in her bonnet; it will protect her now, and later if any of our stragglers should come this way. We shall await the ceremony in silence." Which they accordingly did; and then went into the courtyard where they were regaled with beef, cheese and ale. They went off without the smallest disturbance.

My white cockade was carefully preserved and shown to me from time to time, always reminding me to respect the Scots, and the Highlanders in particular. I think I have obeyed the injunction by spending my life in Scotland, and also by hoping to die there.

Sgd. Rosemary Clerk, Edinburgh

The cockade was worn by Lady Clerk of Penicuik at a ball when George IV visited Edinburgh in 1820. It was later, and with it a piece of plaid which Captain MacDonald wrapped round the child, lost by a granddaughter of Lady Penicuik; and altho' every effort has been used to find it, all attempts have unluckily failed. The piece of plaid is said to have been exhibited in London in the thirties - February or March 1931 - in the house of a Mrs Fleming in Grosvenor Square.

THE WHITE COCKADE

By William Ross (1762 - 90)
A Literal Translation, from the Gaelic

Many a hero and mighty warrior
Are today in Scotland who would follow you,
They secretly shedding tears
Who would eagerly go with you in the strife.

But let our prayers rise early each day
To the Being who is Highest of all,
That we should not foster vengeance
For the injustice towards the White Cockade.

A long farewell to the White Cockade
Till day of doom will not move from death,
The grave has seized the White Cockade
And the cold stones of the tomb is its rest.

CARLISLE IN 1745

By June C. F. Barnes

At the time of the Jacobite uprising, the Carlisle population numbered about 4000, almost all living within the walls, there as yet being little in the way of suburbs outside the gates. The Castle and city Walls had been erected in the reign of Henry I, and the Citadel by Henry VIII, and by mid 18th century all were quite neglected. "An old hen-coop" was how the Duke of Cumberland described the Castle, which was kept by a Governor and a small company of Invalids - semi-retired veterans. However, the closing of the city gates at the sound of the evening gun reminded the inhabitants that this was still a Garrison town, though for over a century it had seen no fighting whatsoever and it was political rather than military battles which occupied the minds of the inhabitants. The principal people in the old town were the Dean and Chapter of the Cathedral and the self-electing members of the City Corporation, who rarely agreed on anything.

The City was not prepared in any way for a siege. When news filtered through of the advance of the Prince's army the Cumberland Militia was mobilised, but on the approach of the Jacobite forces the militia men refused to stay to defend the town and disappeared over the walls in the night, leaving the town to capitulate with hardly a shot being fired.

On the night of 9th-10th November the Prince's army surrounded the town and the Prince spent the night at Blackwell, before moving out to Brampton.

Here he remained for several days: during this time his army occupied themselves in constructing scaling ladders and other siege weapons in the Corby and Warwick woods, and on one occasion the prince was entertained cordially by Mrs. Warwick and her relative, Mrs. Howard of Corby, at Warwick Hall. Their husbands, having suffered sufficiently for the Stuart cause in 1715, kept prudently away. The Prince observed that "these were the first Christian people" he had met with since crossing the border. Here Ranald MacDonald, the son of Tirnadris was brought up, after the execution of his father in 1746.

On November 15th the town capitulated; the Mayor delivered up the keys of Carlisle to the Prince at Brampton, and on November 16th the Corporation attended in state at the Market Cross where King James III was proclaimed. On the 18th they again assembled to greet the Prince as he entered Carlisle, mounted on a white horse and preceded by his hundred pipers.

While living in Carlisle he stayed at Highmoor House, now the site of Marks & Spencer's store. On November 22nd men and women flocked from far and wide to occupy every vantage point on the road to the south to witness his departure as his troops marched past.

20

Four weeks later the Prince returned, now a fugitive with the Duke of Cumberland in close pursuit . . . speaking words of encouragement to the brave men commanded by Col. Francis Townley left behind to hold the town, the Prince left for the North on December 22nd, 1745. The garrison did their best to strengthen the already dilapidated defences with earthworks and sandbags, and fired with what little artillery they had on Cumberland's men, busily erecting batteries on Stanwix bank . . . but by December 27th six eighteen-pounder cannon were able to play on the besieged town . . . by the 30th all resistance was hopeless and the garrison capitulated. The Duke would grant them no terms: only "that they should not be put to the sword, but reserved for the King's pleasure." The prisoners were held in the Cathedral until January 10th when they were sent off to Lancaster. When they were gone the luckless Chapter was left with the unpleasant duty of cleansing and repairing the Cathedral which was left in an intolerable condition of filth. It took six weeks of work renewing the flags and burning sulphur before services could be held there again.

After Culloden the Castle was filled with prisoners, mostly French and Irish troops who had surrendered following the battle. They were later joined by many from Lancaster, Newcastle and Whitehaven who had been returned to Carlisle for trial. Owing to the lack of accommodation in the jail and the Castle, the unhappy men were crowded together in tiny rooms with horrible barbarity. As there were so many to try, the prisoners were offered the option of standing trial, or dividing themselves into batches of twenty amongst whom one was chosen by lot for trial while the others submitted to accept a sentence of transportation. By this means the number of prisoners appointed for trial was reduced to 127. They were separated from their comrades and kept huddled together in one room in the Castle. 96 were condemned to death; these were pinioned in the Castle court, and were seated on a rude black hurdle, with the executioner by their side. The procession slowly passed through the town, outside the English gate to Gallows Hill at Harraby, where the prisoners were hung, drawn and quartered with the barbarous ceremonies which attached to an execution for treason . . . the heads of some of those executed were set up on pikes over the Gates as a warning against rebellions in the future. It was a terrible retribution.

COLONEL FRANCIS TOWNLEY

By T. Fitzpatrick

Francis Townley was born and brought up in Townley Hall, Burnley, which is still quite intact and now used as a museum.

His uncle, Richard Townley, also of Townley Hall, was out in the '15 Rising and was taken prisoner at Preston in 1715 when that town surrendered. He was put on a trial, but found not guilty by a very sympathetic jury.

Francis went to France in 1728 where he made friends with other Jacobites who soon obtained a commission for him in the French Army. He fought under the Duke of Berwick at the siege of Phillipsburg in 1733.

He returned to England in 1742 and lived on a small income in Wales. At the outbreak of the '45, the French king sent him a commission to enable him to raise forces for Charles. He came to Manchester and lived among many Jacobites of the area but had no better luck than did the Prince himself later in recruiting fighting forces. In fact, he offended many by his constant use of hard swearing.

He joined Charles a few days before he came to Manchester and rode into the city with the Prince, who put him at the head of the Lancashire Regiment - small and full of riff-raff though it was.

As everyone knows, Colonel Townley was among the brave men captured at Carlisle. He was tried and found guilty and all through his trial he protested that Cumberland had broken his promise under the terms of surrender at Carlisle, in bringing him to trial. Nevertheless he was executed. His head was placed on the Temple Bar but was removed secretly from there by persons unknown, taken back to Townley hall and buried in the walls of the Chapel there, where it must remain to this day. His body lies in a churchyard in St Pancras, London.

Note: In 1900, Townley Hall became the property of Burnley Council and is now a museum and art gallery. The head of Francis Townley remained in the care of the family and in 1947 found a final resting place with his ancestors in St. Peter's Church, Burnley.

THE MANCHESTER REGIMENT

By Edgar Wyard

The nucleus of this regiment consisted of a small number of English prisoners who had joined the Prince's army after the battle of Prestonpans, but the unit was formed mainly of men recruited in England after the surrender of Carlisle to the Prince, 17 November 1745.

There was little enthusiasm for Prince Charles Edward as he passed through the towns of Kendal, Lancaster, and Preston, but in Manchester, an English ex-soldier, Sergeant Dickson who had joined the Duke of Perth's regiment, had gone ahead of the army and prepared the way in raising recruits in the town and surrounding countryside.

On November 29 the Prince's army entered Manchester midst loud acclamation and the ringing of bells. To please the town, and content all those who were in sympathy with the Cause, it was thought necessary that men who were raised in Manchester should be enrolled into what would be called "The Manchester Regiment". On St. Andrew's Day, November 30, recruits were speedily raised and mustered within the precincts of the Collegiate Church, the focal point of Jacobite sympathy for over a generation.

Prince Charles Edward nominated as Commander of the regiment Colonel Francis Townley of Townley Hall in Lancashire, who had formerly been commissioned in the French Service, and had joined the Prince as he passed through Preston. The officers were obtained principally from the prosperous manufacturing community in Lancashire. Included with them were the three sons of Dr. Deacon, the non-juring Bishop in Manchester. Having joined the Prince's standard they never sought pay either for themselves or their men, maintaining and supporting the regiment by their own means - the colours bore on one side "Liberty and Prosperity" and on the other "Church and Country".

The strength of the regiment, such as it was, never exceeded 300 men. With the rest of the army they marched from Manchester to Derby, and thence back to Carlisle.

Many men had deserted, and now numbering 118, they formed part of the garrison which surrendered to Cumberland, 30 December 1745.

Being Englishmen, they were made the special objects of a bloody revenge. Nearly all the officers and sergeants were hanged, and the men transported. Colonel Francis Townley was executed on Kennington Common 30 July 1746.

Captain John Daniel, in his "Progress with Prince Charles Edward", states that it was never the intention of the Prince to leave the Manchester and Scots

23

garrison to face Cumberland at Carlisle, and that Colonel Francis Townley not only petitioned the Prince in his own name, but in the name of all the officers that they should remain in the city, though they never assented or desired it, many of them wishing to retire over the Esk with the rest of the army.

The Manchester Regiment can claim no "final hour", no "glorious last stand", but at least it had the honour of being the sole contribution of England in rallying to the support of Prince Charles Edward and the Jacobite cause.

EXETER HOUSE, DERBY

by J. Barrie Robertson

It is generally accepted as a fact that when Prince Charles and his army briefly occupied Derby, in December 1745, the Prince lodged at Exeter House in Full Street, and generally agreed that the Council of War of Friday, December 6, which decided upon a retreat, took place within Exeter House.

What is less well known is that the old oak panelling from the interior of the room wherein the Council is reputed to have taken place now adorns the walls of the Committee Room of Derby Museum and Art Gallery. This room is not open to the public, but the keys are in the custody of the curator, who gladly admits visitors on request at his office. On the oak panelling hang portraits of the Prince and some of his adherents, and pictures of old Derbyshire.

When Exeter House was demolished in 1854 the oak panelling of the Council of War room was preserved. In later years Derby Corporation decided to line the walls of the Committee room of the Museum with it and this apartment is now known as the Stuart Room.

SHOULD THE PRINCE HAVE TURNED BACK?

by M. Jenkins

I am a Derbyshire man; and my first acquaintance with the '45 was to be told, at the Crewe and Harpur Arms at Swarkestone, that this was where Prince Charles Edward had turned back. For many years I accepted the fashionable view that the decision to turn back was the one act of sanity in a doomed venture, and that the Prince was a military incompetent. I think that the time has come to revise that view.

The Prince was surrounded by men such as Lord George Murray whose military reputations were of the highest. These men were good soldiers - by the standards of the day; but I believe that the Prince saw that the '45 was not a conventional eighteenth century war and that the military theory of the period was irrelevant to what he was attempting.

Three reasons are commonly given for the return to Scotland: army morale, lack of political support, and the likelihood of military defeat. The last can be discounted. The royal army in 1745 was small even by the standards of the time; it was shoddily equipped, badly led, and poorly disciplined. The best regiments were wasted in pointless continental wars. The average soldier, whether a drunken volunteer or merely pressed into the service, had little desire to fight: he was content to survive and get his pay. Against this pitiful force the Prince ranged a small but highly motivated body whose traditions gave it real battle skill and a lust for combat; it too was undisciplined, but Highland indiscipline showed itself in overeagerness to attack, whereas the English were more likely to flee in panic. It is true that Jacobite morale was lower than it had been; they were an army far from home, involved in the boredom of a triumphal march. A taste of battle would have boosted morale; or London was near enough for the Prince to urge the army on until it scented victory.

The military situation, then, was hopeful; but the political aspect of the rebellion seemed less favourable. The English Jacobites have often been castigated for sitting at home and drinking toasts to the Prince. This was in fact the best thing that they could do. When the Prince came to London he would need reliable men spread throughout the kingdom to look after his interests, and the Jacobite gentry could not add anything effective to his military resources. Jacobitism was widespread. The Whigs made more noise; they had something to lose; but the English Jacobites, understandably cautious in the face of a Hanoverian witchhunt, were by no means a crankish minority. That archetype of Anglo-Saxonness, Sam Johnson, was a loyal Jacobite then, deeply emotionally involved in the Prince's cause.

The loud Whig protests of what fate was planned for the rebels disguised a deep insecurity. The House of Hanover was dull; only those who had profited from it showed any real enthusiasm; and it had involved England in pointless and unpopular continental wars. If few would bestir themselves in the Jacobite cause, equally few would lift a finger to keep King George on his throne. The London mob which cheered for the King today would cheer as fervently for the Prince if the Prince were in London; and the King knew it. That was why the royal family was ready to flee at a moment's notice.

Politically, then, the situation was more favourable than first appeared; but how could it be used? The Prince, I believe, saw that only daring could guarantee victory. Conventional military thinking demanded reduction of enemy forces and establishment of lines of supply - in other words, a slow, cautious advance. But let the army advance rapidly on the capital, uncovered, with a show of confidence - and Whig confidence could well evaporate; the house of Hanover would as usual play it safe and withdraw over the North Sea; and in accordance with the precedent of 1688, the Stuarts would be invited to return.

Perhaps the Prince did not reason thus. Perhaps he acted out of ignorance and folly; but his folly made more sense than his advisers' wisdom. When Murray insisted on the retreat from Derby, he doomed the rebellion; he gave the government time to organise resistance and he robbed his own men of impetus and confidence. It is not surprising that, on Drummossie Moor, the Prince - wrongly this time - rejected the advice of the men whose caution had snatched victory from his grasp.

Jacobite Medal, probably struck in Edinburgh in 1745
(Courtesy of Noel Woolf)

GLASGOW

by Margaret MacKerracher

Glasgow did not favour the Jacobite cause.

At the opening of the Rising the City had raised two battalions of 600 men each, to fight against the Prince. When it was learned that he was in retreat from Derby, and was coming to the City with an army of between 4000 and 6000 men, the worst of treatment was expected. The magistrates had already unwillingly given £5000 in money, and £500 in goods, to the Prince, after the battle of Prestonpans when he was in occupation in Edinburgh. Quarter-master Hay and the Chief of MacGregor had come to collect. The sum asked for had been £15,000 but the Glasgow Magistrates had decided on the restricted amount of £5000, holding that 'necessity was no law.' Glasgow at that time was not a wealthy city. Its whole annual revenue amounted to £3000 and its expenditure to £3081. The arrival of the Highland host on Christmas Day, bareheaded, barefooted, and in rags, with matted hair, according to those who recorded the events of the time, made Citizens of Glasgow quake in their shoes. The famished looks of the army did not help.

The men paraded through the chief streets by devious ways to give the impression of greater numbers, before marshalling at the Cross and proclaiming Charles Edward, Regent of Scotland.

Thereafter the Magistrates were ordered to provide 6000 short coats, 12000 linen shirts, 6000 shoes, 6000 pairs of hose, 6000 waistcoats and 6000 blue bonnets. In addition, the Provost was fined £500. While the garments were being in-gathered, the Highlanders were quartered on the people but it is recorded that they behaved very decently and quietly; so, after all, the visit did not turn out so terrible for the Glasgow Citizens, though the town was left almost bankrupt.

The Prince himself took up his abode in the Shawfield Mansion which was situated at what was then the border between old and new Glasgow. It is said that Charles, together with some of his friends and officers, ate his meals here twice a day in full view of the public. It is further recorded that his appearance was indeed princely, though pale of countenance and dejected and downcast of eye. He dressed more elegantly in Glasgow than in any other place.

Only a few of the Glasgow ladies warmed to the Prince's cause. Notable amongst them was Miss Clementina Walkinshaw whose father, John Walkinshaw, had been one of those who had rescued the Prince's mother, the Polish Princess Clementina Sobieski when, on her way to her marriage, she had been made a prisoner at Innsbruk, in the Tyrol. The rescue is said to have been in a romantic fashion. Afterwards, when Clementina Walkinshaw was born, the Prince's mother acted as the child's godmother, and the babe was given the princess's own name of Clementina.

The Shawfield Mansion no longer stands. It was demolished to make way for Glassford Street, which didn't exist at the time of the '45, the area then being part of the meadows and gardens of the Mansion. At the corner of Glassford Street and Trongate there is now a tall building which houses the Royal Bank of Scotland.

Further along Trongate are the Cross and the 17th Century Tolbooth Steeple with its clock, crown-like spire and chiming bells. There is a tradition in Glasgow that when the Chief of Clan Cameron visits Glasgow on any important occasion these bells will be rung. This is to mark the continued gratitude of the City to his ancestor, the Gentle Lochiel, who at the time of '45 restrained the other chieftains from sacking and burning the city. The custom at one time fell into abeyance but Miss Cameron, the Association's secretary, informed us that her father had revived it, following a period when he had been doing some research in the City Archives, and had discovered the reference to the custom.

St Andrew's church is an imposing building said to be a copy of St Martin in the Fields, London, the chief departure being the steeple, 160 ft high. This church took 17 years to build (1739-1756) but its chief interest for us, was to learn that the greater part of Prince Charlie's army encamped here in 1745. So the first bit of human service that the partly-built walls effected was to shelter from winter the Highland clansmen. It was very near to the Glasgow Green where Charles held a review of his army after they had been refreshed and re-clothed.

Ten days after arriving in Glasgow, Prince Charles and his army marched away again, north-east to Kilsyth. One who followed him and accompanied the army all the way to Culloden was Dougal Graham, the city packman. He was also a rhyming poet and later wrote 'History of the Rebellion' which was considered one of the most valuable accounts of that venture for he had followed the fortunes of the Prince from his army's crossing of the Fords of Frew to the last sad day at Culloden.

THE JACOBITES IN KIRKINTILLOCH

by John Scott

Kirkintilloch is a town which lies six miles to the north of Glasgow and it was through here on Friday, 3rd January 1746, that the Prince passed with his column of the Highland army. Their approach caused much consternation, people fled in all directions taking with them what they valued most.

A young boy called Miller was herding cows on what is now the canal bank opposite Broomhill, and saw the Prince with the Highlanders marching eastwards. Miller lived to be an old man and often repeated what he had seen on that occasion.

A decent woman in Kirkintilloch, when the Highlanders passed through, had a mare in the plough which the Clansmen took with them in spite of the owner's remonstrances. She was determined not to be silenced, however, and followed the army till it halted, when she obtained speech of the Prince, to whom she laid forth the hardship of her case. The Prince ordered the mare be brought to him, and asked the woman if she was quite sure it was hers. As soon as the mare saw her old mistress she neighed and this so convinced the Prince that he allowed them both to depart in peace, and the plucky female rode back on her mare to her own home.

At that time there stood near the Cross, just at the mouth of the 'Kiln Close' a barn, with the gable fronting the street having a 'bole' or small aperture for the admission of air. Farther down the close was a kiln for drying grain from which the close took its name.

The Prince with his men had marched down East High Street but some stragglers remained. A man called Dawson saw a Highlander standing beside the old Cross stone. He went into the barn with his gun, fired at the man through the bole, and killed him. Dawson concealed himself among the straw with which the barn was partially filled, was hunted by five or six enraged Highlanders with drawn swords, who diligently probed all over the straw, but he remained undiscovered.

Meanwhile the alarm reached the Prince who halted his army and threatened to march back and burn the town, the Jacobites seized Bailie Dollar in the Eastside and informed the lairds of Gartshore, Oxgang and Woodhead that all three would hang with the Bailie unless the assassin was given up. The magistrates represented to the Prince that the murder had been committed without the sanction or knowledge of anyone but the assassin himself, and beseeching the Prince for mercy, he was pleased to have the punishment commuted to a fine.

On the Sunday after this event, a solitary Highlander intent on plunder, called at a farmhouse on Cadder estate, and the family being at church and only a young lad left in charge, he decided to help himself paying no attention to the youth's movements. With spirit beyond his years, however, the young lad went out, loaded a gun, and shot the Highlander dead on the spot. As a footnote we should remember the letter in 'The Lyon in Mourning' from Dr Archibald Cameron, brother to Cameron of Lochiel, saying that he prevented the whole town of Kirkintilloch from being destroyed and its inhabitants put to the sword in revenge for the inhuman murder in the town of two of Lady Lochiel's servants eight weeks earlier.

KILSYTH IN THE '45

by John Scott

It was at Kilsyth on the evening of 3 January 1746, that Prince Charles Edward Stuart decided to halt his column of the Highland army. They had marched since dawn on that cold winter morning a distance of 12½ miles over rough roads from Glasgow through Bishopbriggs, Kirkintilloch and hence to Kilsyth.

Prince Charles had been invited to spend the night at the mansion house of the Livingstone Lords of Kilsyth who had always been a staunchly Jacobite family. The mansion house of Shawfield had been owned by the Livingstones up until 1715, when William Livingstone, Lord Kilsyth, lost property and lands for his part in the abortive rising of that year. In 1746, however, the house was occupied by a Presbyterian minister called James Robe, a staunch Jacobite.

The minister was so committed to the Jacobite cause that he bought a sword and a pair of pistols and made ready to join the Prince's Army. He sent his horse to an old Kilsyth soldier to have it battle trained and then took it out to the manse grounds to test it out. When he fired his pistol the horse bolted and threw him to the ground. Most aggrieved, Mr Robe challenged the old trooper that the horse had not been properly broken in. "Broken in!" he replied, "it's as weel broken as ony beast in Prince Charlie's army; bit see, sir, what ye've din, ye've shot 'im in the lug."

CRIEFF

by M. G. Selkirk

Then, on 1st February 1746, the Prince arrived at Drummond Castle on his eventual retreat to Culloden. The following day, he transferred his headquarters to Ferntower House (demolished in 1962), not far from Cope's Well. He reviewed his troops on the Market Park where the Tryst was normally held. This ten acre site is now occupied by Morrison's Academy and its grounds. The Prince appears to have been greatly relieved that the reported desertion from the ranks had been overstated.

His horse needed shoeing, so it was taken to the town smithy in King Street for John Wright, the smith, to attend to it. The Police Station now stands on the site, but let into an outside wall is a stone which once topped the smithy door, showing the owner's initials, the date 1736, a crown and thistle and the tools of his trade, a hammer, horseshoe and a pair of pincers. On 3rd February, Prince Charles Edward held a Council of War in the Drummond Arms Inn, since replaced by a Victorian hotel. To all appearances, the meeting was a stormy one, with blame being hurled about in all directions. Eventually, the decision was taken to split the army into two sections, one to head due north through the Grampian Mountains, the other to follow the coastline past Montrose and Aberdeen. The next day, as the Jacobite army left, after threatening to burn the town yet again, news came that the Duke of Cumberland was hot on its heels. Crieff prepared to mount a loyal welcome to the Hanoverian commander. However, some young men of the town decided that they would go out along the road to give the Duke a greeting of their own. They gathered together some old pistols, pots and pans and, in lieu of a band, some old fifes. Hiding behind a hedge just outside town, they waited until the advance guard came into sight. Then they banged the pans together, blew the fifes and let off the pistols. Unfortunately, only two of the guns actually managed to fire, one of them exploding in the process. The soldiers panicked, thinking that they had run into an ambush and were on the verge of retreating rapidly, when the Duke rode up to find out what the hullabaloo was about. He took the demonstration as a favourable one, scattered a few coins in the boys' direction and said that he hoped their patriotic behaviour would be an example to the other citizens of Crieff. However, he still seems to have been in two minds as to the loyalty of the townspeople, because he left a small garrison behind him, ostensibly to protect Crieff against marauding Highlanders. The local folk must have wondered which side they would have prospered under better when, one day, the soldiers burned down the linen factory which the Duke of Perth had established in 1731 and then cut down all the alder woods on the west of the town for fuel.

31

The Drummond estates were forfeited, but it is perhaps pleasant to record that the income from them was applied to the improvement of Crieff. Ultimately, the lands were returned to the family, who continued to play an important role in the town for many years afterwards.

The silver-mounted targe, said to have belonged to Prince Charles Edward Stuart.
(By kind permission of the National Museums of Scotland)

THE ROUT OF MOY

by Neil MacDonald

On Saturday, 15th February 1746, Prince Charles, accompanied by a bodyguard of 30 men, arrived at Inverlaiden House, near Carrbridge, the home of Grant of Dalrachney. The following morning, a member of the Prince's staff making preparations to bake some bread was observed by Lady Grant who immediately told him that there was to be no baking of bread in her house on the Sabbath day. Whether it was her dislike for the Prince or her Christian principles we don't know, but we do know that the Prince left the Grants' house without further delay. Grant himself was sympathetic to the Hanoverian cause, and was believed to have given Lord Loudoun at Inverness information about the Prince's whereabouts.

The Prince, together with his men, arrived at Moy Hall that afternoon, about ten miles south of Inverness, the seat of the MacIntosh chief. The chief, a captain in the Black Watch in King George's Hanoverian army, was away from home at the time, and the Prince was entertained by Lady Anne, the chief's wife and her sister Margaret who happened to be visiting. They were the daughters of James Farquharson of Invercauld. Lady Anne was a Jacobite and became known locally as "Colonel Anne" for the part she played in recruiting her clan to fight for Prince Charles.

Lord Loudoun, stationed at Inverness with a force of about 2000 Hanoverian soldiers, received information about the Prince's presence at Moy Hall with only a small bodyguard. He called his officers and a cordon of troops was placed round Inverness to prevent any of the inhabitants, most of them Jacobites at heart, from following his movements and giving timely warning to the Prince. On the stroke of midnight, Loudoun quietly left Inverness with some 1500 men and Sir Norman MacLeod, the 19th chief, at the head of an advance guard of 70 of his clansmen.

The Dowager Lady MacIntosh, who resided in Kirk Street, Inverness, had heard of the Prince's arrival at Moy Hall and, her suspicions aroused by the activity of the troops, concluded that some plot to surprise the Prince was intended. Lachlan MacIntosh, a boy of 15, was told to go with all speed to Moy Hall and warn the Prince of the approach of his enemies. Shortly after Loudoun had left the town, the cordon of troops was raised, and the brave lad set out on his journey. He bypassed the army and, on his arrival at Moy, the whole household was alerted.

However, Lady Anne had already taken precautions. Donald Fraser, the estate blacksmith, and four servants were on the alert and took up a position with their muskets about two miles on the Inverness side of Moy Hall. When

Loudoun's army came within earshot, the blacksmith, in a loud voice, gave the order to advance to MacDonalds, Camerons, Frasers etc. and followed this by firing a few random shots. Loudoun's army retreated in great disorder and in the stampede that ensued several men were trampled underfoot. The only person killed that night, however, was Donald Ban MacCrimmon, Piper to Sir Norman MacLeod of Dunvegan, Skye, one of the most famous pipers of his day.

Meanwhile, the Prince was roused from his sleep and retired to a nearby wood.

Lord Loudoun, writing from Dornoch in a letter to the Earl of Stair explaining why he retreated, had this to say: "I thought it improper to march on to a much superior force".

Shortly after the Battle of Culloden, Lady Anne was arrested and imprisoned at Inverness but, owing to her husband's position in the army, she was released in six weeks. When asked to give her reason for supporting the Prince she said, "I believe my country would be happier under its lawful king than under a German usurper".

Donald Fraser, the hero of the Rout of Moy, fought afterwards at Culloden and was one of the few Clan Chattan officers who escaped. He is buried in Moy churchyard, and his sword and anvil can be seen in the museum at Moy Hall.

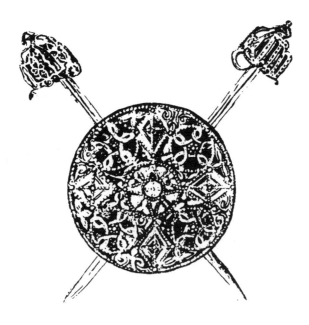

THE BATTLE
OF CULLODEN
WAS FOUGHT ON THIS MOOR
16TH APRIL 1746

THE GRAVES OF THE
GALLANT HIGHLANDERS
WHO FOUGHT FOR
SCOTLAND & PRINCE CHARLIE
ARE MARKED BY THE NAMES
OF THEIR CLANS

CULLODEN

You say that you love Scotland. Have you thought
That Scotland's love must aye be dearly bought?
She calls for deeds, not words; she puts on you
A hard, stern test to prove your love is true.

Could you have firmly stood in line with those
Who, at Culloden, faced their Prince's foes?
Your love for this dear land. Is it like theirs
A Highland love, with which none else compares?

'Tis only in the language of the Gael
That you find words which rightly tell the tale
Of love, borne by these peerless men
To their own homes: to their own Highland glen.

And yet, unhesitant, they left this all
At loyalty's insistent trumpet call.
Could you do this? If you could not - Begone,
Scotland will never own you as her son!

Andrew Murray

THE SIGNIFICANCE OF CULLODEN

by Charles MacKinnon of Dunakin

Surely one of the principal feelings that besets us when we read our first account of the Jacobite rising of 1745 is one of bafflement. From a poor, a decidedly inauspicious beginning, great progress was made. The Highland force swelled into an army, became a first-class fighting unit under an efficient commander, defeated Cope at Gladsmuir and sent him flying to face disgrace and a Court of Enquiry, and Edinburgh the ancient capital fell into the hands of the Prince. This was followed by a triumphant march into England.

And then. . . . .? And then the sudden retreat, the rout of Hawley at Falkirk, another retreat, and finally the chapter of disasters called 'Culloden'.

The words that most readily spring to mind are 'If only'. If only they had forged ahead from Derby to London; if only the night march to Nairn had succeeded; if only they had refused the engagement at Culloden and waited for rest, food and better ground.

Culloden, coming as it does at the end of a series of disappointments, tends to become regarded as the inevitable culmination of a defeat that began at Derby. Yet this is most manifestly wrong. For the startling truth is that the Highlanders were never nearer to complete and overwhelming victory than when, in high spirits, they prepared to engage Cumberland. This does not mean that the time and place chosen for the engagement were good - they were the reverse. But Charles faced Cumberland with two victories behind him and a force of magnificent Highlanders who had not tasted defeat.

First Cope then Hawley had crumpled before the Jacobite onset. Cumberland was very much a Hanoverian last hope, and the Whig government had no other effective source on which to call if he, too, failed them. Had Charles won at Culloden, he would have marched to London virtually unopposed. The 'eating and drinking Jacobites' - those whose enthusiasm was confined to dining clubs - and the Jacobites of England and Wales who had sat on the fence earlier when Charles had still to face Hawley and Cumberland, would undoubtedly have rushed out loudly proclaiming their loyalty to the Stuarts. It is almost impossible to over-emphasise the importance of such a victory to the Stuart cause.

There were, after all, good reasons for the retreats north from Derby and Falkirk. Dealing with Derby first we must not lose sight of the fact that had Charles continued to London he was liable either to be caught up by the numerically superior forces of Cumberland and Wade or else holed up in London. The Prince was anxious to engage Cumberland and then fall on London. Lord George, however, proposed retreat, and the chiefs took his side. Nothing short of an absolute certainty would have justified continuing. Retreat on the other hand was practicable, and Lord George was willing to conduct it. It offered a better chance of ultimate success and would not diminish their honour. We who can be wise after the event, knowing that disaster lay ahead at Culloden, may regret that they did not give battle to Cumberland at this stage.

But Lord George could not foretell Culloden and his advice was sound and his execution of the retreat was masterly. Even had the army successfully pushed through to London avoiding an engagement there was the possibility of London becoming a trap. The Londoners were hostile, the southern Jacobites sitting on the fence could hardly have inspired confidence in their support and aid, and the pursuing armies might have found an easy victim in the trap.

These are but a few of the considerations, but they are weighty enough to indicate how far from foolish was the retreat from Derby.

There can be no doubt that Charles was shocked at the reactions of the English and Welsh Jacobites. He had hoped to swell his army to a force fit to meet the Whig armies on level terms and his disappointment and chagrin must have been great. The march into England was made in the confident expectation of support in numbers. When that support was withheld, and with a pincer movement forming around him, there was every reason for retreating from what began to look uncomfortably like a disastrous situation.

The retreat from Derby, then, is not a mystery but a perfectly reasonable and brilliantly executed move in the right direction - the direction of ultimate victory. And it worked. Charles was able to meet Hawley and Cumberland separately, in the country best suited to his mountaineers and where the vast majority of his active supporters were to be found.

What then of the retreat after Falkirk? Here there was a blunder - not a disastrous one, however. After their victory, some of the Jacobites were for following up and exterminating the remains of Hawley's army. Some were for returning on the march to London. Some maintained that the first job was to take Stirling Castle and so secure easy communication with northern supporters. An engineer, M. Mirabelle de Gordon, was reputedly responsible for persuading the Prince to attack the castle. Too late it was realised how serious were Mirabelle's shortcomings. Three valuable weeks were wasted in a fruitless attempt during which Cumberland came hurrying north. Charles was once again eager to get to grips with Cumberland. But Lord George Murray and the chiefs advocated a retreat further north, partly because the men were dis-spirited after their desertions. They pointed out the obvious advantages of a winter campaign in the north, at which season Cumberland would be at a distinct disadvantage. They could take the northern forts, tire out Cumberland, and in the Spring, reinforced by northern supporters, could fall upon and rout the Duke. Charles was forced to accept this unanimous opinion, although it increased his unjust distrust of Lord George, and the results of a muster at Crieff where it was found that the desertions were much fewer than had been said, did not help matters.

As at Derby, it was not precipitous flight from a victorious enemy. Lord George, like Montrose, knew the advantage of making his enemies follow him on to ground that gave the mountaineers the advantage. These were not the retreats of an army in flight. The Prince and the ordinary clansmen were eager to get to grips with the enemy. Their two victories had whetted their appetite, and it took Lord George much time, and cost him his favour with the Prince, to prevent what he regarded as folly.

And so they came to Culloden - not an army at the end of its tether, but one that had made a brilliant march into England and escaped unscathed. They had two victories to their credit, and when it was learned that Cumberland had crossed the Spey they actually rejoiced at the prospect of coming to conclusions with him.

There are some interesting features. Cumberland crossed the Spey unopposed. The night march to Nairn failed. After this, suggestions (a) to refuse the engagement until food and rest were obtained, reinforcements known to be on the way had arrived and the opportunity was generally more favourable, (b) to fall back south of Nairn water to better ground nearby, and (c) failing both of these to fall on Cumberland before he had drawn up his army properly - all were refused.

At the last moment, the moment of fate, Charles seems to have lost his judgement. Lord George Murray and Colonel John Roy Stewart both urged the three alternatives above and were refused a hearing.

So the army without its reinforcements, with many of its members either in an exhausted sleep or absent on a foraging expedition, on the most unsuitable ground imaginable, faced a numerically superior, rested and well-fed force. Charles seems to have had blind faith in his clansmen. They did not let him down (except possibly on the left wing, but that is not certain and in any case the dice were heavily loaded by now). But they could not accomplish the impossible, and Cumberland's resultant victory meant just as much to the Whig government as Charles's would have meant to the Stuart dynasty. It ended the whole affair.

Why was the Spey crossing unopposed? Perhaps on the whole it was as well that it was. The Duke of Perth has been unjustly censured for not opposing the crossing. His entire force was less than a quarter of Cumberland's and in addition a recent drought had greatly reduced the water level - so much so that the river was fordable in several places and at two of them a whole battalion might have marched abreast. Add to this the fact that Cumberland had a good artillery train, and Perth's actions are at once logical and reasonable.

The night march to Nairn was probably the most fatal step. Had it succeeded, the Jacobite chances of a rout were excellent. There is little cause to suppose that Cumberland would have been able to resist a surprise night attack. Likewise if the march had not taken place, Charles's army would have been rested.

It might have chosen a better spot for the engagement. There would at least have been a sporting chance. But it was attempted and it failed. That was the disaster. The Jacobites returned to Culloden exhausted and frustrated and in no condition to give battle - and this the key battle of the whole campaign. There is not space here to go into all the pros and cons of this march, but on the whole it is perhaps a pity that it was ever attempted. If, as has been suggested, the rear column simply wasn't able to keep pace because the Low country regiments and the French piquets could not negotiate the ground, this might have been taken into account at the outset.

The final folly - and this is real folly - to make a stand on the moor with the army in a pitiable as well as a reduced state, gave Cumberland what he needed to ensure victory. At a different time and in a different place one wonders how the Duke's troops would have faced the dreadful Highland charge. Morale was in favour of the Jacobites had the battle been fought on reasonable terms; their reputation in the fray must have been very much in the mind of the Duke's soldiers, and given a good deal of disquiet even though Cumberland's military reputation was high.

So near, and yet so far. Culloden must have decided the issue one way or the other. It is extremely doubtful if the Jacobites would have had to fight another battle if they had defeated Cumberland. It is nonsense to suggest, as has been suggested, that the Highland attack was outmoded and failed inevitably against better arms and modern tactics. The Whig troops at Culloden had no advantage in either tactics or arms over Cope's and Hawley's troops on earlier occasions. They had no better means of withstanding the Highland attack. What they did have was advantage of terrain literally handed to them and an engagement with an army in no state to do battle.

This then is the true significance of Culloden. It was not the culminating point of defeat. It was the threshold of total victory. Disaster did not begin at Derby or Falkirk as is so often supposed. It began, and ended, at Culloden. And if the fate of Jacobitism hinged on this one battle, so did the fate of the House of Hanover and the history of Britain. A great deal more than is commonly supposed hinged on the inevitable engagement between Charles and Cumberland - as Sir Compton MacKenzie has pointed out, the entire history not only of Britain, but also America and even of France might have taken a different course had the Stuart cause triumphed.

That is the significance of Culloden.

KEPPOCH OF CULLODEN

by Lieut. Col. I. B. Cameron Taylor

It may interest many admirers of Alasdair MacDonell, the 16th Chief of Keppoch who was killed at Culloden, to learn that, when he went to Glasgow University in 1713, he matriculated as MacDonald. However, when he "came down" from the University just before the 'Fifteen Rising', he was MacDonell and this new spelling of his surname has caused some speculation in the ranks of Clan Donald ever since. It would seem that the benefits of a university education were apparent (?) even thus early!

Alasdair MacDonell escaped to France after the failure of the '15, where he completed his interrupted studies and then entered the French military service. he served for ten years, but not as a "foreign mercenary", for Scots at that time had the privilege of dual nationality with the French. he returned home to succeed his father as Chief about 1728 and proved himself an enlightened, far-sighted and vigorous man of affairs. He directed his energies to the bettering of conditions for his clansfolk and the improvement of law and order within his domains.

Keppoch's sword, which is illustrated in "Clan Donald" vol. 11 opposite page 667, has long been the subject of enquiries and was at one time believed to be lost. However, I am indebted to Captain William Mackay, O.B.E., of Inverness, for pointing out to me that the sword is safe and is, in fact, on display as part of the Noel Paton Collection in the Royal Scottish Museum, Chambers Street, Edinburgh.

When the "Keppoch Stone" at Culloden was found again in 1959 and cleared of undergrowth, brushwood and fallen trees, the Culloden Committee of the National Trust for Scotland obtained the Forestry Commission's permission to erect a simple plaque beside the stone.

This reads:-

"The Keppoch Stone

This stone is believed to mark the place where Alasdair MacDonell, 16th of Keppoch, fell mortally wounded while leading his clansmen in their charge during the battle. He was carried from the field and died soon after in a nearby bothy. Aged 49, and greatly lamented, he was known as "The mirror of martial men". 16 April 1746. Seobhag fiorghlan na-h-caltainn."

The line in Gaelic at the foot of the plaque (meaning - "Fearless hawk of the flight") is from the "Lament for Keppoch" which was composed by his bard, Alasdair Cameron, after the battle. Even allowing for the circumstances in which it was written, the whole poem gives a very fair picture of the great admiration and respect which his clan had for this chief. Sir Walter Scott was later responsible for a good deal of (probably inaccurate) historical embroidery on Keppoch's words and actions at Culloden, but this has been successfully unravelled by Andrew Lang in an appendix to his four-volume "History of Scotland".

In the 'Forty-Five Campaign, Keppoch owed his eminent position in the councils not to the strength of his clan, which numbered only 200 at Culloden, but to his upright leadership and sheer strength of character. It is a matter for regret that his great line, stemming from a Lord of the Isles and a Princess of Scotland, should have died out last century. Scotland, and particularly the Highlands, have yet need for leaders of his calibre.

AN OLD STORY ABOUT CULLODEN AND AFTER

by Donald J. Macdonald of Castleton

From a gentleman in Perthshire we have the following tradition of great interest to us, especially to Skye MacDonalds who, although not 'out' in 1745, never refused help to the fugitive Prince as history records.

When the battle of Culloden had been fought and lost and the wounded were being brutally rounded up and murdered, a worthy man Angus MacDonald and his wife Agnes went over the field and found a severely wounded officer of the Clan Donald hidden under a bush where he had escaped from the first rush of the enemy over that area. Before the redcoats returned Angus and Agnes conveyed the officer, who said he was of the Skye MacDonalds, to their croft of Little Drummossie near the battlefield. There they concealed him and nursed him back to health. When the hue and cry had died down, MacDonald returned to his home in Skye and every year, until they both died, he sent his rescuers at Culloden two ponies and as much seed-oats as would seed their croft.

IN THE FOOTSTEPS OF THE PRINCE

by M. Newcomen

Culloden Moor was the starting point for six young men who, in 1986, planned to re-enact the flight of Prince Charles Edward Stuart and his party from the battlefield of Culloden. All participants were wearing the traditional costume of the period which consisted of belted plaids and buckled brogues, and they were also carrying authentic weapons. The group left Culloden Moor on the anniversary of the battle and arrived within five days at the point from which the Prince embarked for the Outer Hebrides. Over one hundred miles was covered without the aid of any modern equipment. Provisions carried on the walk were restricted to food which was available at the time of the Prince's journey.

As I lay in the dark, cold cave, the handle of my dirk kept sticking into my side as I tried to snatch some sleep. I wrapped myself tighter in my plaid, and, as I looked across the cave, I could see my companions by the flickering light of the fire. The night before we had spent in the King's Stable Cottage on Culloden Moor. We had found sleeping on the stone floor cold but it now seemed like luxury, I thought, as I dozed off.

We had begun our journey soon after 1:30 p.m. on Wednesday, 16th April. We marched onto the moor and, as the wind and snow blew into our faces, I remembered that these were the same conditions that the Highland army had faced on the day of the battle. I tried to imagine how those brave Highlanders must have felt. As we left the moor, heading towards General Wade's military road, the weather eased slightly. We crossed the River Nairn at the Ford of Faillie and walked down the single-track road towards Fort Augustus. Our shelter for that night was to be a cave 14 miles from the battlefield. As it grew dark, the wind became stronger and we were soon walking through a blizzard. Arriving at about 6:30 at the cave in which we planned to spend the night, we set about lighting a fire and having something to eat. That night proved to be the coldest night of our entire journey.

We rose at 5 o'clock the following morning without breakfast, descended onto the road and began the 24 mile journey to Fort Augustus. After three hours walking, we arrived at Gorthleck House where we were greeted by Mr. and Mrs. Fraser. A warming cup of tea and a visit to the room in which the Prince had once stayed and then we were on our way again. A long walk lay ahead, culminating in a 4 mile, 2000 foot climb, before going down to Fort Augustus. Some of our party were beginning to complain of sore feet. At long last, we reached Fort Augustus. Loch Ness was at her splendid best, the Knoydart mountains in the background white with snow.

We spent the night in the old schoolhouse and rose early the following morning. Although we were refreshed, the pace was now beginning to tell. By 8:30 we had covered the first part of the 17 miles to Achnacarry. The going was tough and the pace was beginning to slow. We arrived at the ruins of Invergarry Castle around 1:30 pm; a short lunch and we were on the march again. We left the main road and headed towards Kilfinnan Farm and the forest track to Clunes. By the end of the forest, exhaustion was beginning to show. When, as we reached Achnacarry village, a red deer stag was walking towards us in the cold of the evening, even this stirring sight could not lift our flagging spirits and painful feet. By the time we reached the village hall, it was obvious that three of us would be too tired to carry on the following day, as the hardest part of the journey still lay ahead.

We left Achnacarry at around 7:00 am, our party of six now reduced to three, on the long trek to the head of Loch Arkaig. We bathed our feet in the loch and carried on up the glen. At Pean Bothy we were given a cup of tea by a group of students spending the night there. It was now raining heavily. We scrambled up the rocks and descended by a waterfall in order to avoid Lochan Leum. With the wind and the rain in our faces the next three hours' walking were hard going, over wet rocks and muddy terrain. The welcome sight of Oban Bothy lifted our spirits in the dimming light. We lit a fire and tried to dry our clothes. That night was very cold and none of us slept much.

We rose early and set off on the last stage. The weather was breaking up a little as we crossed the Braes of Morar. Tired and hungry, we found it tough going and, at one point, we were travelling at 1 mile per hour. A heavy hailstorm left us soaking wet again. We descended into Glen Meoble and brewed a hot drink in the shelter of an open cowshed. Then began the winding path that would take us over Creag Bhan and down to the west coast.

A mixture of rain and sunshine greeted us as we walked along the road towards Loch nan Uamh. The last five miles proved to be the hardest of the entire trip, but as we neared the beach we unfolded the Standard and, with gritted teeth, we marched as best we could onto the shore. Our friends and a few spectators waited there for us. The journey was over, and a mixture of sadness and satisfaction was felt by all.

We spent that night at the Glenuig Inn, enjoying a hearty meal and a good ceilidh which lasted into the wee hours. As our party broke up to make their own way home, I realised how close we had become during our hundred mile journey, and what touched us all was the warmth and kindness that we received from all the Highland folk. As the Prince said, "I am come home."

WITH THE PRINCE IN THE ISLANDS

by William Currie of Balilone

When Prince Charles landed in Scotland, both Iain MacMhuirrich of Balilone and his youngest son John joined the Prince's Army. Murdoch, the elder son and heir, was commanded by his father to remain in Balilone in Ireland. John, the younger son, fought side by side with his father the 19th Chief throughout the Rising until his father was killed at Culloden. After Culloden John became a hunted fugitive in the Western Highlands.

He was in attendance on Clan Ranald who, along with George Lockhart, younger of Carnwath, joined Prince Charles at Glenbeasdale after their escape from that last battle. Prince Charles prepared to sail to the Outer Hebrides on the 21 April 1746. The names of the gallant little company which served the Prince so faithfully and to whom he owed so much deserve to be remembered so long as the story of the '45 has power to stir men's blood. Among this band was Lachlan MacMhuirrich, one of John's Clansmen. Lachlan was one of the boatmen in the eight-oared boat in which Prince Charles set sail on the 26 April 1746, from Borrodale on the mainland to the Island of Benbecula. For two months Lachlan shared with the Prince all the hardships and excursions the little party endured until they eventually arrived in Lochboisdale in South Uist on 21 June. It was there that they parted and went their separate ways as it had been decided that the best choice of escape lay in the party splitting up. When it is remembered that the wanderings of the Prince, around which so much romance has gathered, lasted altogether five months, it will be seen that Lachlan MacMhuirrich was with the Prince for more than a third of the whole period during which the Prince was a hunted fugitive. Lachlan was made prisoner for helping the Prince to escape to Uist, and taken to London and imprisoned in the house of Dick the Messenger. He was eventually released on the 10th of June 1747. It was on the 21 June that Lachlan MacMhuirrich parted from the Prince and it was on the 28 June that the Prince was taken in charge by Flora MacDonald.

John, the younger son of Iain MacMhuirrich the 19th Chief who was killed at Culloden, had been with Clan Ranald and Prince Charles before the Prince's departure to the Island. John had had several narrow escapes from capture on the mainland. Eventually he was smuggled over to South Uist by some of his own clansmen in the second week of June. As the son of the newly dead Chief of Clan MacMhuirrich, John was given all their assistance to evade capture.

He was in hiding near Nunton, the home of Old Clan Ranald, when Prince Charles and O'Neil, his one companion, arrived and enlisted Flora MacDonald's help to escape. It was John MacMhuirrich who on the 27 June arranged for the six-oared boat to carry the fugitive Prince to Skye and enlisted the remaining oarsmen. Flora with the Prince and Neil MacEachan, a cadet of Clan Ranald and, later, father of Marshal MacDonald Duke of Tarentum, got into the boat manned by John MacMhuirrich and five other oarsmen and set out for Skye after sunset on the 28 June. They ran into a tempest and were unable to keep a regular course, but eventually gained the point of Waternish on the West of Skye. Here they were seen by a party of militia who fired on them. The Prince and Flora lay in the bottom of the boat as the bullets whistled around them. The oarsmen bent energetically to the oars till they got out of reach of their shot and then sailed into a small bay where they rested. They then proceeded to Kilbride Point and landed near Monkstadt, the seat of Sir Alexander MacDonald, at the north end of Skye.

Flora went to Monkstadt to see Lady Margaret MacDonald, who was a staunch Jacobite. She arranged for him to sleep at the home of MacDonald of Kingsburgh and thereafter by the help of certain MacLeods and MacKinnons the Prince was conveyed to the mainland.

When Prince Charles with Flora MacDonald landed at Monkstadt in Skye it was agreed that the boat he had sailed in should return immediately to South Uist. John MacMhuirrich, however, did not go back to Uist with the rest of the boatmen, which, as things turned out, was just as well for they were all captured on arrival. Indeed, MacMhuirrichs from several islands became prisoners, some being transported to the Colonies. John MacMhuirrich, after many adventures, finally reached Ireland and found refuge in Balilone, the house of his brother Murdoch who was now 20th Chief. Despite the dire penalties inflicted on anyone harbouring Jacobite refugees, Murdoch successfully hid his younger brother until 1747, when the General Amnesty was passed for all who had taken part in the Rising.

THE BRAVERY OF RODERICK MACKENZIE

by Sonia Cameron Jacks

One of the bravest deeds of the '45 Rising concerned a young man named Roderick MacKenzie. The son of an Edinburgh goldsmith, when the Standard was raised he hastened to join the Jacobite army, where he became one of Prince Charles Edward's bodyguards.

In the dark days following the Battle of Drummossie Moor, Ruaridh was skulking in Glen Moriston and finding it ever harder to evade the government troops. The people of the glen were suffering bitterly during this summer of 1746, for Cumberland's redcoats seemed to have a special vendetta against them, and young and old were being harried mercilessly. Listening to the soldiers from the secrecy of his cave, his thoughts must have turned to his Prince, dangerously near in a cave high in Coire Dho between Glen Moriston and Glen Affric, and he would, perhaps, have remembered how, on more than one occasion, he had been mistaken for him. At last here was a way in which he could be of real service to his Prince for, realising that escape was now impossible, rather than surrender he would fight and die, and in the dying would endeavour to put the enemy off the scent. The moment of discovery came; the clash of arms was brief, but as he fell Ruaridh cried out, "Alas, you have slain your Prince!"

The redcoats, overjoyed at their good fortune, struck off his head and hastened with it to Cumberland at Fort Augustus. After trying unsuccessfully to trick MacDonald of Kingsburgh, imprisoned there, into confirming that it was the Prince's, the Duke set off for London with his prize. Richard Morison, a prisoner at Carlisle, had been a servant of the Prince's, but he was ill, and by the time he was in a fit state to be taken to London to confirm the identity of the head, it was unrecognisable.

That this delay gave Prince Charles Edward the chance he needed to escape to the west is certain, and there is also no doubt that Roderick MacKenzie's noble deed contributed to that delay. Even at the time this act must have attracted wide notice, for in the "Lyon in Mourning" by Bishop Robert Forbes it is noted that details of the incident should be gathered but, so far as is known, this came to nothing. Roderick's body was buried secretly down by the River Moriston, and the stream nearby is known as Caochan a' Cheannaich, which means Streamlet of the Merchant. During this century his grave has been marked; since 1973 by a simple wooden cross bearing his initials and the date 1746.

THE UNVEILING OF THE 'FORTY-FIVE ASSOCIATION CAIRN ON THE SHORES OF LOCH NAN UAMH 4th OCTOBER 1956

by Marion F. Cameron

Throughout the previous night fierce storms of wind and hail had lashed the West coast of Scotland; and the morning of 4 October - the first snow of winter mantling the surrounding hills and an icy Nor'Wester whipping the dark waters of the loch - augured ill for an outdoors ceremony. Yet shortly after 11:00 am, 200 people were taking their places upon the little promontory which, rugged with heather, rough grass and wind-stunted oaks and junipers, thrust out into deep water and fell from a natural shelf of rock into the Loch of the Caves. From this spot, as had recently been discovered from a living oral tradition, Prince Charles Edward Stuart with some of his devoted supporters, had boarded a French frigate and sailed for France in defiance of the utmost vigilance of his enemies. Only the courage and resource of his adherents and the inviolable loyalty of the people of the district had made possible so audacious and incredible an escape; and today, approximately 210 years later, descendants and clansfolk of the Highland Jacobites had gathered on the same spot to attend the unveiling of a memorial cairn. They came from distant parts of Scotland and England, and two members of the Association present were from Kentucky, USA. Among the local people who attended was Mr. John MacEachan, who had first brought the tradition of this historic headland to the attention of Mr Cameron-Head of Inverailort.

On the crown of the promontory the cairn stood, draped in the St. Andrew's Cross and supporting replica banners of the Loyal Clans.

Shortly before noon, the skies darkened and a savage shower of hail swept the promontory. It was to this wild scene that the pipes heralded the arrival of the Hon. President of the 'Forty-Five Association', the Countess of Erroll, 28th Hereditary Lord High Constable of Scotland, descendant of Lord Kilmarnock who perished on Tower Hill for support of the Stuarts in 1746.

Escorted by her husband, Captain Moncreiffe of Easter Moncreiffe, Unicorn Pursuivant of Arms, and by Cameron of Lochiel, direct descendant of the Gentle Lochiel, Lady Erroll took her place by the cairn. There she was received by Mr. F. S. Cameron-Head of Inverailort, descendant of the Cameron chieftains of Glendessary and by Mr. Seton Gordon, CBE.

Opening the ceremony, Mr Cameron-Head spoke of the strongly Royalist principles of the Jacobites of today, their devotion to the Sovereign, and their joy that now another Prince Charles claimed their loyalty. He welcomed Lady Erroll, who had made a long journey to perform this ceremony and invited her to unveil the cairn.

The Countess of Erroll said that it gave her much pleasure to unveil the cairn, in memory of Prince Charlie and all who were loyal to his Cause. Under her hand the Saltire fell away. The beautiful silk banners of the Clans were lifted from the cairn by representatives of the Loyal Clans and firmly planted in the ground nearby encircling the monument. It was fitting that the Piobaireachd which saluted the unveiled cairn was played by the builder himself, Mr. John MacKinnon, Arisaig.

A bouquet of white and blue flowers was presented to Lady Erroll by 10 year old Simona Howie, Lochailort.

Mr. Angus Macpherson, Hon. Piper to the Association and descendant of James Macpherson, piper to Cluny of the '45, and of a long line of renowned pipers, stepped forward to play his part in the ceremony - a moment eagerly awaited by all who were devoted to the music of the pipes. A grave and dignified figure he paced slowly before the cairn, playing first the groundwork of the piobaireachd, "My King has Landed in Moidart", followed by "The Prince's Salute", and concluding with a special setting of "Lochaber No More", taught to him by his father Malcolm Macpherson, the great piper, seventy years ago. The clear, full, bell-like notes, rising above the sound of wind and waves, proclaimed not only a master of his art, but a spirit in tune with the great days of the past. As the great music swelled, chiming and reverberating through the silence it seemed to have claimed for itself, the rain ceased and wan sunshine briefly touched the scene.

At the conclusion of Mr. Macpherson's performance, Mr. Cameron-Head announced that he would play "Prince Charlie's Farewell to Moidart", a tune composed at the time of the Prince's departure from these shores but since then known only to the members of his own family and preserved by them. Thus, until that day, it had not been heard in public for 210 years. The privilege of hearing this old pipe music was keenly appreciated.

Proposing a Vote of Thanks to the Countess of Erroll, Mr. Seton Gordon recalled that the title of Hereditary Lord High Constable of Scotland had been conferred upon her ancestor by Robert the Bruce on the battlefield of Bannockburn. The only previous occasion during all these centuries that the title had been held by a woman was at the time of the '45 Rising, when the holder called out her Clan in the Jacobite cause. There were those, the speaker said, who declared that they had no sympathy with Prince Charles or with the Jacobites, but this cairn was raised to the memory of men who were ready to die for a cause which seemed good to them and who had scorned to betray the Prince for a reward which, in present currency, would amount to £100,000. It was remarkable, said Mr. Seton Gordon, that the French frigate, together with a companion craft, should have lain openly at anchor in Loch nan Uamh, and remained there in full view for upwards of ten days. The probable explanation was that both ships were flying the colours of the English fleet - which, meanwhile, was vainly searching for them up and down the Scottish coast. While the ships rode at anchor in Loch nan Uamh, a messenger, travelling by night, hastened to a rough shelter high on Ben Alder, afterwards known as Cluny's Cage, where the Prince was in hiding with Cluny and others. When the Prince and his party, also travelling by night, arrived on the shore of the sea loch they found the French ships still awaiting them. And thus the Prince left the spot where the memorial cairn now stands, having brought to the Highlands both disaster and glory.

A local choir sang "Will Ye No' Come Back Again" in Gaelic. Sheets of hail and rain were again sweeping the promontory; but so far from complaining, the crowd seemed exhilarated, as though the harshness of the weather gave them opportunity to realise - and almost in some small sense to share - the hardships of the '45.

Proposing a Vote of Thanks to Mr. Cameron-Head, Lt. Col. D. H. Cameron of Lochiel paid high tribute to him and to the splendid part he had played in promoting and organising this unique ceremony.

The choir sang "God Save The Queen" in Gaelic and the crowd began to disperse.

Those who paused to look backward saw a dignified and simple memorial silhouetted against the Western sea, silence gathering about it but for the sound of wind and water. Embedded in a hidden core of concrete, the strong grey stones had been symbolically laid by Scots at home and in the far places of the world, forming a monument built, not only with traditional artistry, but manifestly with love, and unveiled by a young and gracious lady whose roots sprang from the foundation of Scotland itself. Already the cairn seemed absorbed into and accepted by the landscape, as though it had stood there for ever. So it began that long vigil through storm and sunshine, time and change which will give testimony of Highland courage and faithfulness to generations unborn.

TRIUMPH OF THE HUNTED PRINCE

by I. Cameron Taylor

After the Battle of Culloden on 16th April, 1746 and until his final escape from relentless pursuit at Loch nan Uamh on 19th September of the same year, Prince Charles - despite a government reward of £30,000 for his capture, dead or alive - sought and found his safety in the care of numerous Highlanders of every rank from chief to cateran. Although by no means all had previously been either avid or active in the Jacobite cause, yet in this, one of the greatest organised man-hunts in history, the honour of the Gael and his proud reputation for hospitality to those in need was left untarnished.

In his five months of hiding and moving from place to place, the Prince covered a distance of nearly 800 miles, at first by horse, then in open boats, but mostly on foot. As if in recognition of the amazing fidelity he won, Prince Charles reacted with cheerful heroism, such physical endurance and stamina, such undaunted courage in the face of all adversities - and they were many - that the passing years have not dimmed the lustre of the tale and he yet remains Righ nan Gaidheal and "King of Highland Hearts". Amid the tragedy and sorrow which his defeat had brought upon the country, the Prince's own conduct and behaviour had reached its finest hour.

Although Prince Charles' wanderings covered the Hebrides from South Uist up to Lewis, then Skye, Raasay and Skye again before coming back to the mainland where he travelled as far north as Strathglass and as far east as Loch Ericht-side, yet a mere list of the places where he found shelter is of small account beside the illustrious roll of those who were his guardians and guides: Ned Burke from North Uist, Donald MacLeod - the 'pilot', Donald Campbell on Scalpay, Mrs. MacKenzie of Kildun, Neil MacEachain from South Uist, Lady Clanranald, Flora MacDonald and her step-father, MacDonald of Kingsburgh and his Lady, young MacQueen, Captain Donald Roy MacDonald the younger, MacLeod of Raasay, the MacKinnon chief and John MacKinnon, Macdonald of Morar, Angus of Borradale and his sons Ranald and John, Angus MacEachan of Meoble, Glenaladale and his young brother, Donald Cameron of Glenpean, Donald MacDonald of Glengarry, Patrick Grant and his seven famed companions of Glenmoriston, Roderick MacKenzie - the self-sacrificing hero, MacDonald of Lochgarry, Cameron of Clunes, Captain MacRae, Dr. Archibald Cameron and his brother Donald of Lochiel, Macpherson of Breakachie, Cluny Macpherson, John Roy Stewart, the unknown boatmen, the unswerving but un-named servants, and even those pursuing militia men whose Highland blood proved stronger than their Hanoverian zeal. These names, rather than the caves or shelters or huts or houses, should be remembered for all time and with honour; for many of these men and women suffered cruelly for the aid they gave.

Here, then, the Prince's odyssey ended. Success had at last attended the diligent search for him by his friends abroad, with the French ships and their intrepid skippers and crews. This, the sixth rescue attempt was led by the Prince's Irish former ADC Colonel Warren. At dusk on a Friday evening Prince Charles made his farewells to those he was leaving and stepped into the longboat with his fellow fugitives, to be rowed to the 36-gun frigate "L'Heureux" at anchor in the Loch. It sailed before dawn next morning, on 20 September, 1746.

Bha Bliadhna a'Phrionnsa air dunadh - The Year of the Prince was ended.

THE WHITE ROSE

Descendants of the dauntless, who hoped when hope was vain,
And trusting, never doubted the Prince would come again;
You bear like them, in memory, what no defeat could close,
The flower your children's children will call Prince Charlie's rose.

And who that has not followed, if but in boyhood's dreams,
An upright princely figure; a standard's fading gleams;
And who but still would follow the exile born to reign,
The limp and draggled banner, the hope that challenged pain?

O rest, rest well Prince Charlie, though exiled you may be,
For hearts still pledge in silence, "The King across the sea."
The White Rose may have faded, but still there blooms for you
Around the broken broadsword, the rosemary and rue.

M. D. Cameron of Clunes

THE JACOBITE WHITE ROSE

by M. Smith

Why was a white rose adopted as the Jacobite emblem? An explanation was given in the publication "The True Jacobite", No 9, May 1971.

"Before the Stuarts came to England or sat on Scotland's throne, the rose was a royal symbol; Edmund Crouchback adopted it as his badge from his mother, Eleanor of Provence. This red Provencal rose was transmitted to Edmund's descendants and was used as a badge by John of Gaunt, when he married Blanche of Lancaster. The white rose was first used by Edmund of Langley, Edward III's fifth son and first Duke of York. Thus the white rose of York and the red rose of Lancaster were family badges long before the famous scene in the Temple Gardens, which has been immortalised by Shakespeare (Henry VI, Act II, Scene IV).

When the House of York asserted its rights against the usurping House of Lancaster, the white rose became associated for the first time with the cause of rightful monarchy as such. Later, the white cockade (a variant of the white rose) was worn by the Irish Brigade in French service, and after 1688 the white rose was generally adopted as a Jacobite badge. Jacobites in succeeding centuries carried on the tradition and had a rose engraved on their wine glasses or heraldically on their signet rings."

So, from 1688 onwards, after the departure of King James VII and II to France, the white rose was used as their emblem by the supporters of legitimate, hereditary monarchy, in opposition to usurpers of the Crown whether or not directly appointed by Parliament. The white rose was used as the emblem of the supporters of Prince Charles and the House of Stuart. A further explanation of the use of a rose as a Jacobite emblem in 1745 has been offered by Mrs. M. Grieve in "A Modern Herbal", first published in 1931. "It was the custom to suspend a Rose over the dinner table as a sign that all confidences were to be held sacred. Even now, the plaster ornament in the centre of a ceiling is known as "the rose". It has been suggested that because the Pretender could only be helped secretly SUB ROSA, the Jacobites took the white rose as his symbol."

A white rose, the family badge of the House of York, first became associated with legitimate monarchy in the 15th century, and the same kind of rose was chosen as their emblem in the 17th century by the supporters of King James VII and II, whom they considered their rightful King. Throughout the 18th century the White Rose of York was the emblem of the supporters of the House of Stuart.

The Jacobite rose was the White Rose of York. An anonymous late 16th century portrait of Elizabeth of York, wife of Henry VII, shows her holding the White Rose of York. It appears to be "Rosa Alba", a description of which is given by Nicholas Culpeper (1616-54) in his "Complete Herbal". The flowers are said to be "white and more double or fuller of leaves than the damask or red".

The cockade, worn as a Jacobite emblem, took the form of a stylised wild rose, the "rosa canina", dog rose or wild briar. It is the rose of Lady Nairne's song:-

"There grows a bonnie briar bush in our kail-yard,
And white are the blossoms o't in our kail-yard,
Like a wee bit cockade to deck our Hieland lads,
And the lasses lo'e the bonnie bush in our kail-yard."

A photographic reproduction of a portrait of an officer in Lord Ogilvy's Regiment shows the cockade in the bonnet - a stylised form of the five petalled wild rose.

In January 1969, the Dundee Courier and Advertiser in its "Craigie Column" published information about the Jacobite rose at Fassifern, the home of Lochiel's brother, where Prince Charles stayed after the Raising of the Standard at Glenfiman. "Here a fine specimen of the Jacobite rose flourishes today. How did it come there? No-one seems to know for certain. When the estate passed to West Highlands Woodlands Company, it was found that the roots of the old rose had penetrated the foundations and the task of the new owners was to relax its hold and yet preserve it. The old Jacobite was so firmly rooted that mechanical means had to be used to dislodge it. Could it possibly survive? Time would tell. To the pleasure of its owners, it has survived, and is doing well, thanks to the skill of the local overseer."

The sentiments of those whose emblem was the White Rose in 1745 have been recorded by Lady Caroline Nairne in her song "The White Rose o' June" which ends:-

"Then, O sing the white rose, the white rose o'June,
An' may HE that should wear it, wear Scotland's auld crown!"

JACOBITE STANDARDS

by Barbara Fairweather

Fourteen of the standards captured at Culloden were taken to Edinburgh. One was taken to Glasgow to be burnt. On the 14 June the standards which had gone to Edinburgh were taken to the mercat cross. The Prince's standard was carried by the common hangman and the others by chimney sweeps. They were accompanied by an escort of Lee's regiment. While the Sheriffs watched, at the command of Cumberland, the standards were burnt.

Some which were rescued from the battlefield and carried to safety can still be seen today. Besides these there are stories of others which escaped Cumberland's net. The Stewart banner is probably the best known. This banner is now displayed in Edinburgh Castle and a replica can be seen in the Scottish Episcopal Church in Portnacrois, Appin.

The standard of Lord Ogilvy's Forfarshire regiment is on display in Dundee Museum. After Culloden it was hidden in Logie House near Kirriemuir, Angus. The Cameron standard hangs in Achnacarry, the home of Lochiel. By tradition the bearer was MacLachlan of Coruanan who lived in Mamore. One of the family wrote to the 24th Chief saying that she was emigrating to Canada and offered the banner to the Chief who gladly accepted it. The banner had remained in safe keeping with this family down through the years.

The Macpherson standard is now on display in the Clan Museum, Newtonmore. The Macphersons were not back from the North in time to take part in the battle.

We now consider the 'possibles'. In the National Library of Scotland there is a manuscript by Frank Leslie called "A Jacobite's Who's Who". Mr Leslie writes that the standard of the Duke of Perth which had been carried by MacGruder, the Laird of Comrie, was safely handed to the Duke of Perth before he left Scotland. The Duke died before he reached France. One assumes the banner was used at his funeral. I have not come across any other reference to this banner in any other work I have consulted.

In the book "The Shadow of the Cairngorms" by W. Forsyth, it states that the banner of the Edinburgh Regiment of John Roy Stewart, the green flag of Kinchardine, was taken from Culloden by James MacIntyre and kept safely by him. Once a year, on the anniversary of the Raising of the Standard at Glenfinnan, he took the banner and unfurled it at the top of the Cairngorms. When he was dying he gave it to John Stewart of Pytoulish and as he gave it to him he said, "John, I have sent for you thinking you are the fittest to take charge of what I myself got charge of 40 years ago. It is my dear John Roy's banner. That bravest of men gave it to me on the fatal field of Culloden with his command that nothing but death should separate us. I have kept it ever since, hoping long that its true owner might have use for it and for me: but I am now going the way of all flesh. I can do no more. I entreat you as I have no children of my own, to come when I am gone, and to take delivery of the dear flag from my wife, and I earnestly beg you will treat it with all reverence and care as is due to the gallant soldier to whom it belonged". The banner was preserved by Pytoulish till before his death he presented it to the Duke of Gordon. The Kinchardine mentioned is in the Spey Valley in Badenoch, the countryside of John Roy Stewart.

The standard of Lord Balmerino's Horse was carried into battle by Captain John Daniel who survived unscathed as did the standard. However, it appears to have been stolen from his person sometime during his wanderings and its fate is unknown.

At Mingary, in the little Catholic church in the Moidart peninsula, there is a Glenaladale MacDonald banner. It cannot be claimed to be the actual banner used in the '45, but it is of interest. In the 1745 Association we have a banner which was made during her convalescence from a serious illness and presented to the Association by one of our members, Mrs. Leon Labistour (nee Patricia Newton). It represents the Royal Standard as closely as it is historically possible to make it. No fully detailed description of the standard appears to have been written by any eye witness. Our banner is proudly displayed at each Annual Gathering Dinner.

A MORVERN HERO

by Alastair Livingstone of Bachuil

Donald Livingstone was about 18 years old when he fought at the Battle of Culloden in 1746. His parents were John Livingstone and Anna MacInnes, who are buried in Morvern in the old churchyard above Lochaline. Their grave is marked by a well sculptured recumbent stone, bearing a coat of arms. This was erected by Donald, their son, some time after 1757. He has a place in Highland annals as the rescuer of the Stewart of Appin Banner after Culloden.

At the Battle of Culloden the Appin Regiment which numbered about 300 men was led, not by the young Chief of Appin, but by his uncle Charles Stewart of Ardsheal, who was a noted swordsman as well as a Jacobite leader. The Appin men with the men of Atholl and the Camerons formed the right wing of the Prince's Army and their desperately valiant initial charge achieved considerable success. But they were checked by a vastly superior weight of cannon and musket fire and were forced to retire. The Appin Regiment alone cost no fewer than 92 dead and 65 seriously wounded. Their standard-bearer, one of the Ardsheal Stewarts, was killed at the outset and about a dozen other members of the regiment who carried the banner in their turn were mown down.

In Morvern, Donald Livingstone was known as Domhnull Molach or "Hairy Donald" as he was tough, strong and hairy. After the rout of the Highland army had begun, Donald saw the Appin Banner lying on the ground. Turning back under fire to where it lay, he quickly removed it from its pole. Wrapping it round his body he then joined his retreating clansmen. Sometime after the battle, when the Jacobite cause was clearly in ruins, the Prince gave orders for his Highlanders to disperse to their clan lands. On his way home, Donald suddenly came upon an enemy officer who was fishing in a stream and who struck out at him with his fishing line. The hook caught in Donald's nose (Livingstones to this day have long noses!) but Donald cut the line free with his dirk and despatched the officer. Many colourful stories are told about Donald's later activities, his epic swims between Mull and Morvern and his encounter with a whale and a shoal of herring, but space does not permit of these being related here.

The Banner was later delivered by Donald to the Stewarts of Ballachulish. This family held it until 1930 when the Stewart Society acquired it. At an impressive ceremony in 1931 it was deposited for safe custody in Edinburgh Castle. The Banner is made of thin blue silk with a yellow saltire, or St. Andrew's cross. Part has been cut away, not perhaps by Donald's dirk but more probably, it is said, "by the scissors of one of the Ballachulish ladies" whose tender heart would melt when she looked on the blood-stained threads. All Jacobite colours captured at Culloden were burnt in Edinburgh "by the hand of the common

56

hangman, with many suitable marks of indignation and contempt". Donald Molach's place in clan history is therefore due, not merely to his having rescued the Appin Banner but to his having saved it from an ignominious fate and contributed towards its survival today.

Donald eventually became tenant of the change-house (or inn) at Savary, Morvern. By this time he had a family consisting of more than four children. Some of his descendants and also descendants of his brother Hugh (Eoghan Ban) are traceable today. A strong tradition links Donald's forebears with Lismore and Appin - also with those of Dr. David Livingstone. Certainly Dr. Livingstone has recorded that his great grandfather "died at Culloden fighting for the old line of Kings". Unfortunately he does not tell us the Christian names of his great grandfather nor does history record the Christian names of the four Livingstones killed at Culloden. So Donald and David have left the field open for their family links and history to be traced by keen genealogists!

Editorial Note

Sir Dugald Stewart of Appin, Brigadier Iain Stewart of Achnacone and Alastair Livingstone of Bachuil recently organised the placing of a memorial plaque to Donald Livingstone in Kiel churchyard, Lochaline, beside the gravestone of his parents. Beneath the heading "A Morvern Hero", it bears the inscription - "This Donald Livingstone (Domhnull Molach) born 1728c died 1816c at Savary, Morvern, rescued the Stewart of Appin regimental banner at Culloden in 1746. The banner is now in Edinburgh Castle. This memorial plaque was placed here in 1982 by Stewart, Livingstone and other clansmen."

THE COLOUR THAT GOT AWAY

by James D. Boyd

One of the most interesting exhibits in Dundee's City Museum is the colour made for, and carried by, the 2nd Battalion of Lord Ogilvy's Forfarshire Regiment at the battles of Falkirk and Culloden.

The Earl of Airlie was out in the 1715 Rising and for his part in that, his title and estates were forfeited. The loyalty of the Ogilvys to the Jacobite cause was not diminished by events and so we find the Earl's son and heir, David, Lord Ogilvy, rallying to Prince Charles' cause in 1745. He raised a regiment in his native Angus, representative of his tenants, douce Dundee citizens and others who held the old Royal line of Scotland in high regard. Before he left with his regiment to join the Prince at Perth, Lord Ogilvy made arrangements for a 2nd Battalion to be raised under the command of Col. John Kinloch of Logie. This 2nd Battalion was charged with certain duties in Angus and Dundee and thereafter to join up with the Prince's army as soon as possible. The 2nd Battalion was soon formed and went into action. A detachment was despatched to capture and hold the town of Dundee in the Prince's name.

Dundee Town Council and a majority of citizens had been pro-Jacobite in 1715. James VIII rode through the streets of Dundee and the two bells of the ancient Steeple (St. Mary's Tower) were cracked by over enthusiastic ringing by Jacobite supporters. In 1745, however, the Town Council were not Jacobite sympathisers and so the men of Lord Ogilvy's Regiment took them prisoner and locked them up in their gaol in the Adam's Town House then just thirteen years old.

The Colour of the 2nd Battalion of the Forfarshire Regiment was a labour of love and patriotism by two Jacobite ladies of Arbroath, named Mudie. The colour is of silk with hand woven linen edging. The Forfarshire Regiment beat an orderly retreat from Culloden and made its way south over the mountains to disband in Angus. Lord Ogilvy and his lady eventually escaped to France, but Cumberland wreaked vengeance on the county of Angus which he regarded as a 'hotbed of rebels'. The Colour was taken from its pole and hidden away in Logie House near Kirriemuir, the house of the Kinlochs.

Years later when the vengeance of the anti-Jacobites had abated, the Colour was taken out of its hiding place and displayed in a special case made for it. In 1921 Logie House and its contents, including the Colour, were up for sale. The Flag was purchased for £750 by a Glasgow antique dealer. Sir John Henderson Stewart of Fingask House, Perthshire, bought the old Colour for £1000 and presented it to Dundee Museum.

The Colour was collected by the then Curator of Dundee Museum, Dr. Millar, who returned in triumph with this ancient proud battle flag and, with a flourish, spread it over a table placed in one of the art galleries before an assembled company. This was more than mere theatricals because the table in question is one that came from a well known building in Aberdeen, once known as 'Cumberland's House or Lodging', Cumberland's requisitioned HQ before Culloden, where no doubt he issued many of his cruelly repressive orders against those who had fought for the Prince. By Cumberland's order, captured 'rebel' colours were burned by the public hangmen of Edinburgh, Glasgow and Stirling at the Mercat Crosses of these towns. Dr. Millar had a sense of justice when he spread the Colour of the 2nd Battalion of Lord Ogilvy's Forfarshire Regiment over the Cumberland table. This Colour, after many adventures, did have the last word.

THE GREEN BANNER

by Roderick Clarke

Among the many historical relics on display at the Clan MacPherson Museum at Newtonmore are the clan's Green Banner and the Black Chanter of Clan Chattan. The Green Banner was carried at the head of the Clan in the '15 and the '45. It is of dark green silk and bears the Chief's arms emblazoned in gold upon it.

It is related that before the Battle of Culloden an old witch or second-seer told the Duke of Cumberland that if he waited until the Bratach Uaine (Green Banner) and the Feadan Dubh (Black Chanter) came up he would be defeated. Ewen of Cluny and six hundred other MacPhersons fought at Prestonpans and accompanied Prince Charles into England. During the retreat from Derby, they put two regiments of Cumberland's dragoons to flight at Clifton and fought valiantly at Falkirk.

In the weeks before Culloden they invested Atholl Castle and guarded Drumochter Pass should the government forces choose to come north by that route. The word to gather at Culloden came to them late and they were on their way there from Badenoch when fugitives from the battle told of that sad day's disaster. It has always been said that the MacPhersons never lost a battle when An Bratach Uaine was present with the chief at their head.

WEAPONS OF THE '45
(from a longer article on weapons used during the Jacobite Risings)

by Norman H. MacDonald

One of the most notable pistols was the all-metal Scottish one which first appeared around the close of the sixteenth century. The main difference was the stock which was made of either brass or steel instead of the usual wood. The butts of many had fish-tailed ends and were sometimes of wood with brass or silver mountings.

The standard cavalry sword carried during the Forty-Five was a backsword. It had a straight single-edged blade and a full basket hilt, the pattern of which was determined by the colonel of each regiment. The blade was usually 31½ inches long and 1⅛ inches broad.

Around 1700, captains and lieutenants of the foot regiments carried pikes and ensigns half-pikes, but by 1710, captains had espontoons and lieutenants half-pikes. In 1743 all infantry officers were directed to carry 'spontoons and this practice continued until their abolition in 1786. Sergeants carried halberds during the whole period and in fact until 1792.

By 1715, the claymore or great, two-handed sword, had entirely disappeared from the battle-field and had been replaced by the basket-hilted broadsword. Most of the blades appear to have been made in Germany, although the Gaelic bards sing of the fine Spanish blades and the name of "Andrea Ferrara" captured the imagination of Sir Walter Scott. Ferrara was a swordsmith who worked in Belun, near Venice, in the sixteenth century, but the blades which bear his name are of seventeenth and eighteenth century manufacture. The name of Ferrara, therefore, merely indicated a mark of quality. Many blades carried the words "Prosperity to Scotland and No Union". The hilts were generally made in Scotland and by the beginning of the eighteenth century Scottish hilt-makers had acquired a considerable reputation for craftsmanship. Swords were also manufactured in the Highlands and many of the more powerful chiefs had their own smiths and armourers e.g. the MacRuaries to the MacDonalds of Sleat. Two excellent examples of the period from the Clanranald Collection are on display in the Scottish National Museum of Antiquities in Edinburgh. One has an iron hilt inlaid with silver and bears the date, 1716. The other has an elaborate basket-hilt of French design and is said to have been presented 'to Prince Charles Edward by West Highland Jacobites.

The Lochaber axe appears to have been given its name simply because it was the type of pole-axe used in the Lochaber district. The blade had a hook at the back which could be used for dragging mounted men from the saddle prior to despatching them.

The targe or buckler usually consisted of two layers of wood covered with cowhide and studded with nail heads in circular patterns with an arm strap and hand grip on the reverse side. The usual size was about 20 inches in diameter. A detachable spike was often fitted into the centre as a defensive weapon. Many fine targes can be seen in the Scottish National Museum of Antiquities where there is a most beautifully decorative one described as "The Prince Charlie Targe". In the Royal Scottish Museum, Edinburgh, is the handsome targe of Alasdair MacDonnell of Keppoch, killed at Culloden, perhaps the finest surviving targe of all.

The average length of the dirk was about 18 inches. This was a hunting knife in time of peace and a stabbing weapon in time of war.

The "sgian dubh" or black knife worn nowadays in the right stocking is a comparatively modern innovation possibly introduced by Colonel Alasdair Ranaldson MacDonnell of Glengarry either as part of the uniform of the regiment of Fencibles which he raised during the Napoleonic Wars or at the time of George IV's visit to Edinburgh in 1822. It superseded the oxter knife, a small knife formerly concealed in the armpit by the Highlanders.

THE SCOTTISH HIGHLANDER'S TARGE

by P. A. Daybell

"The Lord's my Targe . . . . " begins John Roy Stewart's psalm, and there are a few other historic allusions to targes, though not very many nor very descriptive, just a mention. The earliest I have found is contained in the Prologue to Chaucer's "Canterbury Tales", written about 1387, in his description of the wife of Bath - " . . . . and on hir head an hat, As broad as is a bokeler or a targe . . . . ". Later references can be found in books written in the 1600's and 1700's, for example Daniel Defoe in "Memoirs of a Cavalier", written about 1721 but describing the Highlanders forming part of the Scottish Army invading England at the start of the Civil War, states " . . . . and they carried great wooden targets, large enough to cover the upper part of their bodies . . . . ". Possibly the final comment was that of Boswell in 1773, " . . . . There is hardly a target now to be found in the Highlands. After the Disarming Act, they made them serve as covers to their buttermilk barrels, a kind of change like beating spears into pruning-hooks . . . . ".

What then is, or was, this target or targe? The anglicised form of the word is derived directly from the Gaelic "targaid", meaning "a shield". This weapon was carried by the Highlanders during the 15th to 18th centuries as an integral part of their military equipment. It was always circular, about twenty inches in diameter, and was constructed of two layers of oak or pine about ¼" thick, fastened together with nails, glue or wooden dowels, so that the grain of the timber in each layer ran at right angles to the other layer. This method added greatly to the strength of the finished article and might be considered to be an advance form of the lamination as used in modern plywood. The ½" board thus produced was covered with leather or skin, both back and front. Bull or cow hide was used mainly, though sometimes deer or goatskin might cover the back, occasionally still carrying the animal's hair.

The front of the targe was decorated, frequently, and especially in the earlier periods, with elaborate tooling of the leather, using geometric designs and also the typical Celtic interlacing patterns and sometimes stylised foliage, animals and birds. Brass or iron nails were employed originally to supplement the tooling, but these were developed to form the basic pattern, with tooling as 'infilling' only or omitted altogether. The patterns again were geometric - concentric circles, radials, roundels, stars, triangles and arcs; in most cases very subtly used. Later developments in design introduced the use of brass strips and plates, often pierced and engraved and sometimes backed with coloured material such as red felt, as in the basket-hilt of a broadsword.

Almost all targes carried a central boss. This might range from a large brass nail with a 1" head to a pierced and engraved brass hemisphere some 3½" across. Frequently these bosses were constructed to hold a steel spike, which might be up to 12" or more in length. Smaller bosses were often placed at the centres of roundels and, by careful integration with the pattern and the use of larger sizes of nails, would add a richness of effect to the composition. When all forms of embellishment were employed together - tooled leather, brass nails, pierced brass plates and bosses backed with red felt - then a most handsome setting indeed was provided for the fearsome spike.

The back of the targe would be fitted with one or more straps of leather, a hand grip, a gauntlet sleeve of leather, in various combinations, to enable it to be carried on the forearm when in battle. A leather thong was also attached to allow the targe to be carried at other times, slung over the shoulder. A narrow leather sleeve or pocket would house the centre spike, which would be unscrewed from the boss and thus carried for safety when not required for fighting. The weight of a completed targe was about 4 to 5 pounds, possibly heavier if many nails were used - some patterns number between 800 and 1000.

So much, then, for the description of the targe. It is unfortunate that because of the perishable nature of the main materials used, wood and leather, very few ancient targes have survived. A handful of nails and a boss may be all that will be found in the ground, whereas, for instance, swords and dirks may be recovered almost intact.

The famous book by R. R. MacIan, "The Clans of the Scottish Highlands", contains some interesting observations on targes, and his illustrations, now perhaps better or more widely known as 'MacIan prints', feature quite a number of targes though in most cases the pattern is not discernible. These drawings do, however, show very clearly how the targe was carried over the shoulder and how it was held during fighting. The targe was not just a protective shield; it was very much a weapon of offence in close fighting. The spike was an obvious offensive feature, but in addition the targe was used to catch and hold an opponent's blade so that, by forcing it aside, an opening was created for the Highlander's thrusting broadsword. This usage is somewhat akin to the use of a cloak wrapped around the forearm in 'cloak and dagger' fights, of 'main gauche' dagger and rapier, and a further comparison is that the dirk was sometimes held in the left hand protruding forwards at the side of the targe.

There is a story about an English soldier and a Highlander at the battle of Killiecrankie. The Highlander took all his adversary's blows on his targe, but managed to land some cuts on the Englishman who was so enraged that he shouted, "You dog - come out from behind the Door and fight like a man!" Surely the targe was being used at its defensive best!

Another story of a battle, Culloden this time, suggests that, having thrown away their targes to lighten their burden on the previous night's march and abortive attack, the Highlanders were rendered much less effective in the ensuing engagement. However, John Prebble in "Culloden" states that the efficacy of the Highlanders' combined use of broadsword and targe had been consciously countered by the enemy by special training - "In the weeks since Falkirk, however, the infantrymen had been trained to thrust his bayonet at the exposed under-arm of the clansmen attacking his comrade on the right and to trust presumably, that his comrade on the left would do the same service for him."

These comments lead to an interesting speculation - how far can the loss of the battle of Culloden be attributed to the diminished effectiveness, whether through absence or counter-measure, of the Highland targe?

JACOBITE GLASS

by F. Peter Lole

There are probably between 1-2000 examples of Jacobite Glass still extant today, possibly more than any other type of Jacobite memento. I am sure that most of you know that it is the decoration which makes Jacobite Glass Jacobite, not the glass vessel itself, with one possible exception. In the early 18th century quite a lot of glasses had a bubble of air trapped in the stem and as the stem was pulled out the bubble became pear-shaped and is always referred to as a 'tear'. There is a Jacobite tract of 1714 in the British Library having a little couplet in it which runs: "At the sad prospect of His people's woe, Let the big tears in our goblets show." Some people argue that all glasses like that are Jacobite, but I think that that is stretching it a bit.

When you get down to what are undoubtedly Jacobite Glasses there are two forms of decoration. The great majority of it is engraved and there is a tiny minority of painted coloured enamel decoration. There are two types of engraved decoration; what I call the 'mainstream' is wheel engraving and there is a much smaller group of diamond point engraving. For wheel engraving you need a treadle-operated lathe driving a little copper wheel which is fed with an abrasive and the design is actually cut into the surface of the glass. It is a very skilled and definitely professional craft and the equipment is not especially portable. The other form of engraving is diamond point, which is simply done with a diamond stylus, which looks just like a 'biro' and is completely portable; most of it is amateur. A very nice example came up for sale recently, inscribed just below the rim, "God bless PC and down with the Rumps." There is, however, one group of diamond point engraving which is very definitely professional and which is wholly Scottish; these are the 'Amen' Glasses. We will come back and talk about them later on.

When we come to look at the emblems which were used on Jacobite Glass, above all it is the Rose with one or two buds. About 10% also have a thistle. But a writer on Jacobite glass remarked: "There is not a flower that blows that has not been laid tribute as a Jacobite emblem"; I think carnations, honeysuckle and forget-me-nots probably are Jacobite. In addition to the Rose we very often meet an oak leaf or a radiant star, a butterfly or a moth and occasionally a bee. Something like 15% of the Glasses have portraits engraved on them; 99% of those are of Prince Charles, usually but not always, based on the Robert Strange tartan portrait.

Quite a lot of Glasses, in addition to all that, have mottoes or toasts in either English or Latin. There are two Latin ones, out of some twenty-five, particularly worthy of mention. One is the word 'Fiat' which occurs on over one-third of the Glasses, the Latin word which means 'let it be', or 'it shall be' and is entirely the same as the Greek word 'Amen'. The other motto, which occurs more often than not on the Portrait Glasses, is 'Audentior Ibo', which means 'I shall come more boldly' or 'I shall return more boldly', and coupled with Prince Charles' Portrait I do not think that needs any explanation.

When one comes to look at the emblems in general, there is complete lack of agreement amongst the experts about what they do mean. That is probably not surprising when you remember how scattered and diverse the Jacobite movement was and how independent and often cantankerous the Clubs were. I think that in those circumstances it is unlikely that there would be uniform agreement about what they all meant. The Rose with its one or two buds is far and away the most important of the emblems. Some say it simply represents the Stuart Cause, some say it represents the English Crown. Some take the two or three elements which occur together, the Rose with either one or two buds, as representing James, Charles, Henry in varying combinations. This probably is the most widely accepted theory, but I cannot make any single one of the theories which attribute personal allusion fit the chronology of the majority of the Glasses, and my own belief is that we should take the rose to mean the joint representation of the Stuart Cause and the Crown. It is worth commenting that when you meet a Rose on a Glass it usually has six petals, occasionally seven, sometimes eight. Almost never does it have the five petals which a true heraldic Rose should have and which, strangely, all the other Jacobite representations of the Rose do have. Why the Glasses are different no-one has a theory about.

When the Glass has a Thistle it used to be argued that it indicated a Scottish Glass. It has become abundantly clear that when you look at the group of Glasses where we have a provenance which goes back to at least the last century, the proportion of these which have got Thistles is higher in the English group than it is in the Scottish group. Nowadays, one of the few things on which we mostly agree is that where there is a Thistle with a Rose it simply represents the twin Crowns of England and Scotland, particularly so since the Thistle and the Rose are often dimidiated - an heraldic term which means that they both spring from the same stem; occasionally you get springing from the same stem all the flowers I have mentioned, Roses, honeysuckle, carnations and forget-me-nots.

There is another unique feature about Glass which you don't meet in the other relics, for with ceramics or medals, prints or pamphlets, the Hanoverian or anti-Jacobite examples are at least as numerous as the Jacobite ones, frequently more numerous. With Glass the Hanoverian is outnumbered more than ten to one by the Jacobite examples.

Where did all this Glass come from? Dr Geoffrey Seddon has brilliantly photographed almost 500 of the 'mainstream' Glasses and by comparing the engraving characteristics I think he very convincingly demonstrates that two-thirds

of all that group of Glasses come from only five engravers. The earliest record of wheel engraving in Britain is from the early 1730's and I think probably till about 1760 it was very much concentrated in the London area. You certainly meet advertisements in provincial newspapers from 1750 onwards for engraved Glass, but very often those early advertisements talk about "best London engraved glass". Engraving was done not in the Glasshouse, but in separate workshops and some of those by 1760 had become quite large. We have got a probate inventory for one London glass cutter and engraver who died in 1765 and his stock at the time of his death was almost 15,000 glasses.

My belief is very definitely that a majority of the early 'mainstream' Glass came from the London area. This view, that the earlier Glass, which is much the bigger group, was predominately southern in origin, I think is supported by the fact that when we look at the group of between two and three hundred Glasses whose ownership we can trace back into at least the last century, there are fewer 'mainstream' Glasses, known as being in Scotland then, than there are of the 'Amen' Glasses, which are themselves regarded as very rare, but which we know all to have been Scottish.

The most vexed question of all is that of date. I think that we can be fairly confident that few if any of them occurred before 1735 and that the majority were done before 1760, but which side of 1745 they were made is totally unclear and arouses great passion. There does not appear to be any contemporary written evidence at all to help us. Geoffrey Seddon has put forward a well argued case for a majority preceding the Forty-Five. But we have got a very good dated series for Jacobite Medals, thanks to Noel Woolf, and if you look at the seven years before 1745 no medals were issued, whilst in the seven years 1745-1752, fifteen were struck. That would certainly argue that Jacobite mementoes were post '45, which is my own, albeit contentious, view about the Glass. However, Jacobite Glass continued to be produced through the second half of the 18th century, throughout the 19th century and right up until today, and I am not speaking of the fakes, but of Jacobite Glass produced because people want it.

The usage of the Glass: what was the effect on the ordinary clansman? As far as glass was concerned, the effect was absolutely nil. By the mid 18th century window glass and bottles were fairly commonplace, but drinking glass was still very much the perquisite of the monied minority rather than the working majority. We have two nice diary memoirs of mid 18th century Scottish ministers, both of whom talk of the single glass going round the table with the bottle. Then there is the celebrated First Statistical Account from Banff which talks of, in 1798, one bottle being drunk from twelve glasses, whereas fifty years before twelve bottles were drunk from but a single glass. So possession and use of Jacobite Glass I think was a gentry and nobility thing. Many of the explicitly Jacobite Clubs met in private houses and some of the hoards we know of in private houses are quite large. The biggest I know of is a hoard of thirty Glasses still in the house in which it seems very likely they were first installed over two hundred years ago. In Scotland the hoard sizes are smaller - the biggest I know of in Scotland was that of Lord Torphichen in the Lothians who had nine, and Traquair and James Steuart in Edinburgh each had seven.Two other features about the use of Glass deserve comment: firstly, the question of toasting over the water. There is one very good reference, of 1746, to a large bowl of water in the centre of the table; the gentlemen all stood, extended their Glasses over the bowl and toasted 'The King'. There is a widespread belief that finger bowls were used more circumspectly to do exactly the same thing, although there is no contemporary reference to this happening. Secondly, to what extent were the Glasses smashed after the toast was drunk? There are several 18th century accounts of glasses being smashed, but often in rather rowdy circumstances and I doubt very much if best engraved Glass was often deliberately smashed.

In conclusion, I now return to the 'Amen' Glasses. There are 35 of these known, all of them Scottish. For many of them we have a history which goes back into the 19th century and, in a few cases, into the 18th century; usually only a single 'Amen' Glass was owned by a family. Half a dozen of them cropped up within fifteen miles of Stirling including one at Airth Castle. In form, all of them are diamond point engraved, so that the decoration is just linear and is essentially calligraphy. All of them have the J 8 R, James VIII of Scotland, cypher on them. Most of them have between one and four verses of the Jacobite version of the National Anthem, finishing up with the word 'Amen', hence obviously the name of the group. We can be fairly confident that they have all come from a single engraver. He may well have been itinerant and engraved them in the owner's home, but there is some very sketchy evidence that he may have worked in the Edinburgh area. The 'Amen' Glasses have some fascinating and important differences from the 'mainstream' Jacobite Glass.

First of all they all have the J 8 R cypher and the 'mainstream' Glass hardly recognises James, being Charles orientated. Four of them are dated: 1743, 1747 and two in 1749. Quite a number have secondary dedications on them - Wm. Drummond and the Bank of Scotland, Lochiel, Traquair, the Earl Marischal and The Faithful Palinurus; almost a third of them also have a dedication to Prince Henry. Furthermore, quite a number of them come from families who still hold to the Roman Catholic faith. They are a most interesting group of Glass on which much fruitful work remains to be done.

LADY OGILVY'S ESCAPE

by C. W. H. Aikman

After the Battle of Culloden many of the officers and men made their way to Ruthven in Badenoch where they expected to receive instructions from the Prince. Amongst those who went to Ruthven was Lord Ogilvy who commanded the Forfarshire Regiment. He was accompanied by Lady Ogilvy and during their stay they resided at the house of Mr. Gordon of Killihuntly near by.

Their being nothing now but dispersal, his Lordship marched his men across the mountains from Speyside to Dee-side in Aberdeenshire and over the hills by the Capel Mounth into Glen Clova to home territory. Unfortunately, not long after her husband had left Ruthven, Lady Ogilvy was taken prisoner by the enemy. She was first taken to Inverness, then was sent to Edinburgh Castle on June 15th to keep company with the Duchess of Perth, Viscountess Strathallan and Mrs. Jean Cameron. Lady Ogilvy was a brave, handsome and ready-witted woman. She was not confined in prison so strictly that her friends were unable to visit her and while they were making useless efforts to obtain her release she determined to effect it herself. Unto this end she decided to use as her agent a little, ugly, deformed woman with a peculiar hitch in her walk who brought her clean linen every week. As she was leaving the room after one of her usual visits, the captive detained her, saying she had a very strong desire to ascertain if she could walk as she did, would she mind showing her how it was done?

Although very surprised at the lady entertaining such a whim, the old woman readily gave the requisite lesson, and then took her departure. Lady Ogilvy practised the step until she thought she was proficient. She told her friends who prepared everything in readiness to aid her flight when once outside the Castle. Then the day came when she decided to put the plan into operation. The old washerwoman made her appearance as usual and Lady Ogilvy persuaded her to change clothes with her and said, "Do you remain quietly here; no one will harm you, and you will save my life". Then, taking up the basket, she assumed the old woman's limp, left the room and joined the wash-girl waiting outside the door; together they went down the stone stair, out into the yard, passed through the gate unchallenged by the Sentinel, and quietly walked out of sight. The girl was surprised at her mistress's silence, but attributed it to the fact of her sorrow for the prisoner she had just left, but her surprise was all the greater when she saw the crooked little creature throw away the basket and reveal herself as a tall, majestic woman running down the High Street as fast as her nimble feet could carry her.

Lady Ogilvy made her way to Abbey Hill where she found her friends anxiously waiting her with a change of dress and horses. The escape took place on 21 November 1746. However, she still had to endure much hardship, before

70

reaching the Continent. A journey on horseback to rendezvous with a Dutch ship in the Firth of Forth sailing out from Leith was frustrated due to severe weather. The master of the vessel had agreed to heave to in Prestonpans bay and pick up a party of Jacobite fugitives including Lady Ogilvy. They had a boat provided for their use from Newhaven to meet the Dutch ship. This was a sore disappointment for they had to make their way back to Edinburgh and had to take refuge in a fisherman's hut for a couple of days before travelling back to the capital.

It was not until Christmas Eve that Lady Ogilvy, dressed in male attire and posing as a sick gentleman, set out in a chaise for London attended only by Archibald Hart, an English merchant, who brought her safely to London. Upon endeavouring to get over to Holland from the English coast, she was seized upon by an officer and his party who were searching for Prince Charles Edward. The gentleman who was with her acted his part so well, that he convinced the officer that it was a lady of rank in men's clothing, who had run herself so deep in debt that she disguised herself as a man to get abroad and save herself the disgrace of being thrown into prison. This ended the long journey from Ruthven in Badenoch to the English sea port from which she embarked for France and her husband. Lady Ogilvy died in exile at the age of 33 years.

The weather vane Prince Charles Edward erected
on the Palazzo San Clemente in Florence

THE ENIGMA OF SIMON, LORD LOVAT

by B. S. Hart

In Fraser country, the ruined Beauly Priory is the ancient burial place of the chiefs of the clan. In the early eighteenth century a new mausoleum was built at Wardlaw on the opposite side of the river from Beauly, and it is here - or is it? - that the decapitated body of Simon Fraser, Lord Lovat, was laid to rest after his execution at the Tower of London on 9 April 1747.

Lovat made it known that he wished his body to be taken to Scotland and buried in the family vault, and the House of Lords, the authority in charge of such options, raised no objection.

After the execution, the body and head were handed over, as had previously been arranged, to Lovat's Edinburgh lawyer, William Fraser, James Fraser, an apothecary of Craven Street, Strand, and Stevenson, an undertaker who provided the coffin and 'herse'. It was expected that the coffin would shortly be shipped to Scotland and that this would be the end of the Lord Lovat episode.

But on 13 April, General Williamson, Deputy Governor of the Tower of London, wrote, scandalised, to the Secretary of State, the Duke of Newcastle, that the two Frasers and Stevenson 'to my great surprise . . . have been making a show of the body for money, of which I complained to Lord Cornwallis yesterday, and desired that he would acquaint your Grace of the great indignity, as well as indecency of it, a thing never before heard of." The upshot was that the undertaker was ordered to return the body to the Tower forthwith, permission for its removal was countermanded and it was interred in the Tower chapel of St Peter ad Vincula near to the bodies of the Lords Kilmarnock and Balmerino, whose executions had taken place the previous year.

This should have been the end of the story, but nothing relating to Simon Fraser was ever quite straightforward. Although, over a hundred years later, when restoration of the chapel was taking place and three unidentifiable bodies, presumably those of the three Lords, were found, rumour grew and persisted that a substitute body had been buried in the Tower, while that of Lord Lovat had been smuggled to Scotland and, as he had wished, been buried with his forebears at Wardlaw. That this is what really happened is given credence by the discovery at Wardlaw earlier this century of a lead covered wooden coffin and detached from it, a short distance away, a copper tablet whose laudatory Latin inscription proclaimed that the remains within were those of Simon, Lord Fraser of Lovat.

Definite proof may be lacking, yet it does not seem unlikely that, after the turmoil of his wayward life, Lord Lovat was still capable of pulling a fast one and that, as he wished, he lies at peace among his ancestors and the chiefs of his clan.

HUGH MERCER AND LORD PITSLIGO'S HORSE

by Malcolm G. Selkirk

In the *Oxford Dictionary of National Biography*, there is an entry for a Hugh Mercer who, it is stated, served as a surgeon's mate in the army of Prince Charles Edward Stuart, afterwards escaping from Culloden to America.

His name does not appear in the Muster Roll, but there is a brief note of him in A. & H. Tayler's book, *Jacobites of Aberdeenshire and Banffshire in the 'Forty-Five*. However, there is no indication as to the regiment with which he served, or to the surgeon whom he assisted. Accordingly, I decided to see if I could track down Hugh Mercer's origins and his role in the Uprising of 1745. An American museum also expressed interest in my research, as did the Local History Department of the North-East of Scotland Library Service and, after five months of trips to Aberdeen, North-East Scotland and Edinburgh, I was able to put forward my theories. I admit that there is no hard evidence as to Mercer's participation in the '45, but I believe that the circumstantial evidence is credible.

Hugh Mercer was born in 1726 at Pitsligo, near Fraserburgh, a son of the manse. He was a descendant of Andrew Mercer of Aldie, the great Perthshire family, who had been granted lands in the North-East in 1381. He received an education at Marischal College, Aberdeen, graduating from there as Master of Arts in April 1744. The next documentary evidence we have of him shows that he sailed from Leith to Philadelphia in the second half of 1746. What happened in the intervening eighteen months is a mystery, as far as written records go, but let me make an educated guess.

If, as we are told, Hugh Mercer was a surgeon's mate in the Jacobite army, it is reasonable to think that he had already received some medical training. The curriculum of Marischal College at that time, shows that Medicine and Chemistry were taught in the final year of the four-year MA course. As Mercer later set up in business as a doctor and an apothecary, clearly he must have been given more training than that single year's session. The usual method, in the 1740s, was for graduates to continue their professional studies with an established medical practitioner, assisting him and learning at the same time. So, who did Hugh Mercer turn to for his medical schooling? The records are blank, but I believe that his natural choice would have been his own family's doctor.

Dr John Cruickshank was a native of Ellon, who first set up practice in Fraserburgh shortly before Hugh was born. He seems to have been the only doctor in the immediate area and was certainly well-known in that part of the Buchan countryside. He may even have encouraged the young Hugh to pursue a medical career, having known the boy since birth.

When the call came from Prince Charles Edward for his supporters to rise and help him claim the throne of Great Britain for his father, the response from North-East Scotland was mixed. A number of key people who had been 'out' in the 1715 Uprising refused to take the risk again, but Alexander Forbes, 4th Baron of Pitsligo, thought long and hard until he eventually decided to cast his lot once more with the Stuarts. It was no easy decision; he was 67, frail and asthmatic. However, once he had plunged in, he sent word to all his relatives and friends to join him. To say that he was respected in the district would be an understatement. He was revered and loved. No-one had a bad word for him. His distant connection, old John Gordon of Glenbucket, pounded through the glens, raising a Jacobite force by means of threats and, even sometimes, kidnapping. All of Lord Pitsligo's men came willingly and out of devotion to the man.

Dr. Cruickshank of Fraserburgh, Pitsligo's own physician, was one of those volunteers. Did he bring Hugh Mercer along with him? Let us examine the known facts.

Mercer was born and lived for the first nineteen years of his life at Pitsligo Manse, a mere twelve minutes' walk away from Pitsligo Castle, the home of the aged Alexander Forbes. His father was the minister of the parish, having arrived in 1720, soon after Lord Pitsligo had returned from exile in France, following the abortive 1715 Uprising. The minister was a regular visitor at the Castle and Lord Pitsligo and his family worshipped in the little church, now a ruin. It can be safely assumed then that Hugh Mercer and Lord Pitsligo were well acquainted.

A mile away, and visible from the manse, stood Pitullie Castle, the home of William Cumine, who was also a volunteer with Lord Pitsligo's Horse. He married his Lordship's niece in the small church just before the Uprising and was, indeed, little older than Hugh himself. They would have known each other all their lives, as well.

Other acquaintances included the Ogilvie brothers of Auchiries. Their father had died whilst they were still young, so the older boy and the two younger twins were made wards of Lord Pitsligo. All three volunteered for service with their guardian as soon as his call came.

Another, more mature, man who responded was Thomas Mercer of Auchnacant, near Ellon. He became Lord Pitsligo's aide-de-camp and remained at the older man's side throughout the campaign, even going into hiding with him in the most trying circumstances, after Culloden. More to the point, Thomas Mercer was a cousin of Hugh's father. He lived in Aberdeen for most of the time, where he was an important merchant and the chances are that when Hugh was studying at Marischal College in the town, the two would have met reasonably often.

Throughout the North-East of Scotland, the principal landowners were interconnected by ties of marriage. The Cumines, Moirs, Gordons, Irvines, Thomsons, Ogilvies, Douglases and Mercers who joined Lord Pitsligo in the great

74

adventure were all tied by some form of kinship. Does it not then seem reasonable to suggest that when Lord Pitsligo called for a Troop of Horse to be raised, would Hugh Mercer have joined any other regiment? His father's cousin, his neighbours, his friends, even former fellow-students at Marischal, were all answering the call to arms. Who else would he prefer to go with, especially as he could use some of his newly-acquired skills in medicine for their benefit?

I have examined all of the 36 regiments in the Prince's army. Half were Highland clan regiments, a few were made up of Scots exiles in France, one from England and the remainder were raised mainly in specific districts. Of the three regiments from Aberdeenshire and Banffshire, Stoneywood's and Lord Lewis Gordon's were infantry and raised later than Pitsligo's, which was a cavalry regiment. None of the recruits to the first two named came from the Pitsligo area. In fact, the nearest was recruited thirty miles away from Hugh's home.

I also looked into the backgrounds of the two dozen or so medical men who fought with the Prince's army and, apart from Dr. Cruickshank, I could find no reason to connect any of them with Hugh Mercer.

I have stressed that Pitsligo's was a cavalry regiment because this has some bearing on Hugh's later life, as we shall see. The Jacobite cavalry, all seven regiments, probably never exceeded 800 in number at best. By the time of Culloden, only about 100 mounted men could be brought to the field of battle. The Prince's cavalry was never designed for the traditional charge; it was neither heavy enough or numbered enough. Instead, it was employed to reconnoitre and patrol. It also covered the retreat of the main infantry all the way back from Derby, a feat which most authorities regard as being the most admirable and efficient action in the entire campaign.

After Hugh Mercer escaped to America, he volunteered for service with British troops in trying to stem the advance of the French into the Colonial States in the 1750's. Later, he became a close friend of George Washington, whom he had first met in the battles against the French. They were neighbours in Virginia too, and when the American Revolution began, Hugh joined Washington as a brigadier-general. At his friend's recommendation, Congress put Hugh in charge of a flying column of horse, a highly mobile troop which could reconnoitre, then pounce on the enemy and, just as quickly, melt into the countryside. What else is this but a description of Lord Pitsligo's Horse? I believe that Mercer's experience during those few months of the Uprising, stood him in good stead in America.

Sadly, he died of his wounds after a battle at Princeton in 1777. He was . not quite 51. more than 2,000 people are said to have attended his funeral, so he must have commanded great respect. Perhaps some of Lord Pitsligo's character had rubbed off on him.

His son became a colonel in the US Army and his grandson was a Confederate general in the Civil War. To carry on the military tradition, a direct descendant of Hugh Mercer's daughter, was the World War II general, George S. Patton.

I hope that this brief history, extracted from a much more detailed study, persuades you to agree with my theories about an unusual man who was primarily a doctor, became a soldier by force of circumstance, but was also a Jacobite.

THE SILENT PEOPLE

by Mairead MacKerracher

In the wake of the ruin of the great houses who supported the Stuarts there came many unknown and unsung victims of the new Acts and harsh measures taken to prevent any recurrence of Jacobitism. These people were not the heroes and martyrs who died bravely and left behind them a multitude of witness, both in their own words and in the hauntingly beautiful songs and music that have travelled the world over. They were what was known as the "Sma' Folk" - the people who lived dependent on the great houses and the established order of things.

Greig Among these was a man named John Greig, an Aberdeenshire fisherman from the village of Cairnhilly, near Fraserburgh, who at the time of 1745 was engaged in the trade of salt herring; but the Salt Tax made it hard for him to prosper, as he was not in a salt-panning area. Accounts of John Greig differ. Some say that he was non-political, others that he fought at Culloden - a battle in which his Chief and many of the name of John Greig, or Gregg, took part. Although it would be rash to jump to definite conclusions, certain facts would seem to bear out the active Jacobite theory: in 1746 John Creig felt forced to leave Scotland and follow his trade of fishing abroad, and many years later his great-great-grandson applied for, and was admitted to, membership of Clan MacGregor.

On his arrival at the Norwegian port of Bergen - where he had intended only a temporary stay - John Greig found it financially advantageous to remain there, realising that an untapped source of wealth lay in the fine large lobsters in the deep cold waters of Norway. He set up an exporting business, and prospered. He married in Bergen and had a son, Alexander, who married a Norwegian girl, Margaretta Hertinem. Unlike his father, Alexander had none of the exile's longing for home. He was a native Norwegian, but held British nationality and acted as English consul in Bergen. At his wife's request, he changed the spelling of his name to Grieg.

His son, Edward (Edvard Hagerup Grieg, 1843-1907), lived through yet another revolution - this time absolutely civilised and without bloodshed. Norway voted herself out of the Northern Alliance and, the menace of Russia now gone, Sweden reluctantly agreed to let her go. The Norwegians were jubilant to be a free nation again, though reluctant to accept the great nineteenth-century geniuses their country produced. Edward Grieg fought their prejudices and eventually he became the first great composer to write in a true Norwegian style.

Burnes Another who became a displaced person of his times was the Earl Marishal's gardener at Inverurie, a man named Burnes. With the loss of his employers, and as a known Jacobite, it became necessary for him to leave home and seek work elsewhere. Taking his family with him, he eventually settled in Ayrshire. There he held to his strong Jacobite convictions and passed them on to his family, along with a great respect for learning.

The family name was changed to Burns by his son, a very upright, hard-working man who, however poor he himself might be, always tried to obtain a good education for his family. For this pursuit of literacy we have much reason to rejoice, for it was his son, Robert Burns the world-famous poet, who rescued the old traditional songs of Scotland before they were altogether lost.

The 1752 Medal, origins and significance uncertain
(Courtesy of Noel Woolf)

THE THREIPLANDS OF FINGASK AND THE '45

by C. W. H. Aikman

Dr. Stuart Threipland was the elder son of Sir David Threipland of Fingask and was 29 years of age when he and his younger brother, David, joined the Prince in 1745. Their father, Sir David, had forfeited his estates in the 1715 Rising and had lived in France as an exile for a number of years. Dr. Stuart graduated in medicine from Edinburgh University in 1742 and was admitted a Fellow of the College of Physicians two years later. He inherited the baronetcy on the death of his father in 1746.

David joined the Perthshire Horse, but his career was to be cut short. When in pursuit of some dragoons after the Battle of Prestonpans one of the dragoons turned round and, seeing only a lone horseman chasing them, he pulled up and shot David.

Dr Stuart became chief medical adviser to the Prince. He accompanied him to Derby and back to Scotland and Culloden. The medicine chest which he carried with him is said to have been brought by the Prince from France. It contained a pestle and mortar, a number of surgical and writing instruments as well as 158 different medical preparations. This medical chest is now in the care of the Royal College of Surgeons, Edinburgh.

After Culloden, Dr. Stuart parted from the Prince and he went into hiding with Cluny and Lochiel. The latter had been badly wounded in both legs. They were in hiding in Badenoch, then Dr. Stuart left there some time in July to make his way to Edinburgh. He met up with one William Gordon, a book-seller who disguised him as an apprentice. They made their way to London and Dr. Stuart travelled on to France and Rouen where he joined a notable party of exiled Jacobites which included Sir Robert Strange, the engraver, William Hamilton of Bangour, the poet, and Andrew Lumsden who was afterwards the private secretary to the Prince.

Dr. Stuart, or rather Sir Stuart as he now was, returned to Edinburgh after the amnesty was declared in 1747. He became a well respected member of Edinburgh society. He married twice, first in 1753 Janet Sinclair, Caithness, and second in 1761 Janet Budge-Murray, another Caithness lady. He had two children by his first wife and six by his second. In 1766 Sir Stuart was elected President of the Royal College of Physicians until 1770.

Fingask estate which had been managed by the York Building Company after its forfeiture in 1715 was put up for sale in 1783 by its creditors and Sir Stuart bought it back. He died at Fingask at the age of 89 in 1805. He died as he had lived, a true Jacobite.

THE CAPTAIN'S HALFPENNY

by Michael Sharp

I have been fortunate in coming across a halfpenny of George II of the type struck during the years 1740-1745, the reverse having been smoothed and engraved "Captn. Andw. Wood of the Rebel Army Gave me this Halfy July 28 1745 while Confind Wm. Stapley."

It should have been dated 1746. This human error, presumed the result of association of thought with the '45, combined with the patination of the piece, serves to underline its authenticity.

Andrew Wood was a shoemaker of Glasgow appointed, as a burgess, to the roll of shoemakers on 7 June 1744. It was said that he 'took on with the rebels' on 28 December 1745, two days after the Prince had arrived in the City and ordered its magistrates to provide 12,000 shirts, 6,000 coats, 6,000 pairs of stockings and 6,000 pairs of shoes for his army. Macbeth Forbes states in *'Jacobite Gleanings from State Manuscripts'* that Andrew Wood made shoes for the rebels in Glasgow, was greatly in debt and was offered a captain's commission in the Jacobite Army. His indebtedness would seem in doubt, however, since other accounts state his commission as having been dependent on his being able to raise a company of fifty men from his own pocket. Andrew Wood, duly commissioned, joined Colonel John Roy Stewart's Edinburgh Regiment. The Edinburgh Regiment apparently guarded the baggage train at Stirling when the Battle of Falkirk was fought and yet both Colonel Stewart and Captain Wood are reported as having fought in that battle. The Regiment fought in the front line at Culloden where Captain Wood was taken. He was promptly imprisoned at Inverness and was brought to London in June and confined in the prison hulk 'Thane of Fife' before finally being taken, presumably shortly before his trial, to the New Prison at Southwark.

He was tried at St. Margaret's Hill and many testified against him stating that they had (variously) seen him armed and in highland clothes wearing a white cockade, beating up for volunteers, with his company, with his Colonel and on the field at Falkirk. He was duly condemned whereupon he petitioned for mercy, stating that his grandfather, a lieutenant colonel, had commanded five hundred men in the Revolution, his father had taken the government side in The '15 and that he himself had been instrumental in effecting the escape of nine men of Glasgow who had been captured by the Prince's army. An affidavit dated 22 September 1746, bearing the seal of the Corporation of Glasgow and signed by various people in the presence of the Lord Provost, was presented in support of that last claim. The Captain's plea was ignored and he was sentenced to death.

On the eve of his execution he sought spiritual comfort from a cleric of the Presbyterian Church, in which he had been born and raised, but did not find this forthcoming being instead charged by him with the most horrid crimes. Captain Wood quickly found the solace he sought when received into the Church of England by Bishop Gordon, a non-jurant Scotsman resident in London. The following morning, the morning of 28 November, Captain Wood was taken to Kennington Common where some of his comrades had earlier been despatched. This choice of location was probably deliberate, Cumberland holding the Lordship of Kennington and his spite knowing no bounds. Captain Wood was 'haltered' with the red and white rope, called for wine, which was readily provided by the prison drawers, drank the health of the rightful King James III, read his scaffold speech and was then, in the words of the time 'turned off'. Mercifully he was allowed death at the rope's end before the remaining and barbaric aspects of his sentence were carried out. He had not reached twenty-one years of age.

Unfortunately, nothing is known of William Stapley or the circumstances in which he was given the halfpenny. That he had it engraved as a memento shows that his encounter with Captain Wood left a lasting impression on him.

EBENEZER OLIPHANT - A JACOBITE SILVERSMITH

by B. S. Hart

Amongst the equipment abandoned on the battlefield in the confusion after the Jacobite defeat at Culloden was Prince Charles Edward Stuart's baggage wagon. Speaking of this sometime later, James Gibb, master of the Prince's Household, mentioned that together with linen, cutlery and other goods lost was "the Prince's hunting equipage in a shagreen case, consisting of six silver goblets, doubly gilt, going into one another, two knives, two forks and two spoons, all silver and doubly gilt". He regretted "the loss of the hunting equipage more than that of all the rest, for . . . it was one of the most curious things he had ever seen in any place. The Prince brought it with him from France." Gibb had heard that it had fallen into the Duke of Cumberland's hands and that he had despatched it from Inverness to London as a great curiosity.

This can only be Prince Charles Edward's silver camp canteen, a unique treasure which has now returned to Scotland permanently after two hundred years, bought for the nation as the result of a public appeal.

The Duke of Cumberland is said to have presented this 'great curiosity' to Lord Bury, son of the Earl of Albemarle, his chosen emissary to carry the news of the Hanoverian victory to King George II in London. It remained in the possession of the Albermarle family until about twenty years ago. Due to recent publicity the appearance of the canteen has become well known and so has the name of the Edinburgh silversmith who made it - Ebenezer Oliphant. It is thought that the camp canteen was a twenty-first birthday present to the Prince from Scottish Jacobites and as Ebenezer Oliphant was the son of a family staunchly loyal to the Stuarts, no better choice of designer and craftsman could have been made. His mark EO is on the silver with the date 1740-41.

Ebenezer Oliphant was the youngest of the fifteen children of James Oliphant, laird of Gask, and his wife Janet Murray; he was born at the House of Gask on 17 March 1713. The rather unlikely choice of Christian name may have been taken from that of a celebrated preacher of the time, Ebenezer Erskine.

As certain careers - the services, the church and the law - were debarred to Jacobite families, younger sons of lairds, unable to make a good living on the land, frequently became merchants or tradesmen and so it was that young Ebenezer at the age of fifteen was apprenticed to James Mitchelson, a leading Edinburgh goldsmith with premises in the Parliament Close. He served his time with Mitchelson and in August 1737 he became a master goldsmith himself - a Freeman of the Incorporation of Goldsmiths of Edinburgh. His cautioner, or sponsor, on that occasion was an Edinburgh bookseller, William Drummond - Oliphants and Drummonds often lent each other friendly support.

For some time from about 1738 Ebenezer Oliphant was in partnership with Dougal Ged, and it was Ged as Assay Master who stamped his mark on the Prince's canteen.

Although his eldest brother Laurence, Laird of Gask, and his nephew, also Laurence, both joined the Prince's army, Ebenezer did not come out in the '45. However, on at least one occasion during the campaign he was able to help his young nephew. Laurence, an ADC to the Prince was sent to Edinburgh with news of the victory at Prestonpans. Some Hanoverian dragoons fled back to the city after the battle and seeing the young officer with only a civilian companion fired their pistols and slightly wounded him; one of them tried to corner him alone in a close and would have attacked him - Ebenezer, however, grasped the soldier, saying "What want you, friend?" whereupon the assailant 'snaked off'. A man of peace - and consequence.

Ebenezer suffered no penalties for his Jacobite sympathies and his business prospered; so much so that in 1753 he was able to make a substantial contribution towards buying back the Gask estate which had been forfeited after the Rising and to restore it to the family. His own home in Edinburgh seems to have been the meeting place for them all on their visits to the city. For many years he was an office bearer at Old St. Paul's Church, which he attended with his wife, Amelia Belches of Invermay, and their five children. Amelia died in 1779 and both she and their children pre-deceased Ebenezer who in his old age was cared for by one of his nieces.

Aged 84, Ebenezer Oliphant died in 1796 and was buried where his wife and children lay in Greyfriars churchyard. Their grave is now unmarked, but Ebenezer is remembered for the splendid gift he made for his Prince - a witness to his loyalty, and his skill and mastery of the exquisite craft he followed.

PORTRAIT OF A JACOBITE CHIEF

by Charles MacKinnon of Dunakin

Having been attainted for his part in the Rising of 1715, he was "out" in 1745, at the age of 63. On 13 October, in response to an appeal from Charles by letter written from Edinburgh, MacKinnon with upwards of 150 men, in company with Raasay, joined the Prince near Edinburgh. MacKinnon was the only Skye clan chief who supported Charles in the attempted restoration, his powerful neighbours the MacLeods and the MacDonalds pursuing a more "prudent" course. MacKinnon left Edinburgh on 31 October and crossed into England with the army on Friday, 8 November. When the army marched from Carlisle to Derby the MacKinnons and the MacDonalds of Glencoe had each been joined by 20 more of their clansmen, which is a notable exception to the prevailing desertions which took place about that time.

Ian Dubh led his men through England, and on the retreat, and they fought at Falkirk on 17 January 1746. They accompanied the Duke of Perth into Sutherland where they routed Loudoun. Part of the force, probably commanded by Captain John MacKinnon of Ellagol, Ian's nephew, were with Lord Cromarty on the expedition to recover £12,000 and stores from the captured Jacobite vessel "The Prince Charles". They were in Sutherland on 16 April, when Culloden was fought. Ian Dubh, however, seems to have returned with the remainder of his force, along with the Duke of Perth and rejoined the army, for he is one of the chiefs who attended the council held on 15 April - the day before the fateful battle.

At Culloden, Ian Dubh and his men fought beside their old allies, the MacLeans, in the centre of the front line and afterwards were among the 2000 men Lord George Murray rallied at Ruthven. A letter from Charles, however, dispersed this force. Nonetheless Lochiel was determined to carry on with the plans to regroup the scattered forces and Ian was one of the chiefs who planned to meet at Lochiel's home, Achnacarry, on 15 May 1746. But the attempt failed because few, if any, of the chiefs were able to reach Achnacarry.

On July 4th Charles was brought by Malcolm MacLeod to Ellagol, where he sheltered with the family of Captain John MacKinnon of Ellagol. Charles at this time was posing as Lewie Caw, the son of a Crieff surgeon, and John's wife remarking on his condition said, "Poor man. I pity him but my heart warms to one of his appearance!" She was taken into the Prince's confidence, as was her husband who returned home shortly afterwards.

The Prince was anxious to conceal his presence from old Ian Dubh who was 64 at this time. Doubtless His Royal Highness felt that one so old would prove more hindrance than help, but John was unable to conceal the information and Ian hastened to greet his Prince. Lady MacKinnon of MacKinnon prepared a feast in a cave where they entertained the Prince before setting out that night for the mainland.

After skulking in the neighbourhood of Loch Nevis, where on the 7th they had an alarming encounter with a party of redcoats, Ian and John brought the Prince to Clanranald's house. Clanranald refused to receive him, so they passed on to MacDonald of Morar where they had a similar reception.

The Prince was so downcast that he turned to John MacKinnon and said, "I hope, MacKinnon, that you will not desert me too and leave me in the lurch."

Falling on his knees with tears of indignation in his eyes, the venerable loyalist cried, "Never will I leave your Royal Highness in the day of danger but will, under God, do all I can for you and go with you wherever you order me."

The Prince was so moved that he hurriedly assured Ian that he was mistaken in taking the remark as applying to himself. Thereupon John MacKinnon followed his uncle's lead and made the most earnest protestations of loyalty. These were not empty vows. Charles is reported to have narrated this incident years later to the Pope, when in Italy, and the Pope apparently expressed himself as strongly impressed by the MacKinnons' faithfulness.

On 16 July they brought Charles safely to Borrodale where they handed him over to the protection of the MacDonald chieftain of that name. On the following day both Ian Dubh and John were taken prisoner. They refused to give any information, although John was threatened by Captain Ferguson with a flogging, and one of the clansmen who were with them was stripped, tied to a tree and flogged till the blood spurted from both sides. When threats failed, they were put aboard the "Furnace" and eventually taken to Tilbury.

Despite the rigours of that infamous voyage, old Ian Dubh stood up well to hardship when younger and stronger men died daily. Ian and John were put in the Tower together and there they lay till 1747 when, at the end of the year, they were tried. Both were pardoned, Ian in view of his advanced age and his so-called "mistaken" sense of chivalry.

Before he left the court, Sir Dudley Ryder, the Attorney General, called Ian back and asked him, "Tell me, if Prince Charles were again in your power, what would you do?"

Undismayed by this unexpected challenge, or by the fact that his pardon might be in jeopardy, the old man replied boldly, "I would do to the Prince as you have done this day to me. I would send him back to HIS OWN country!"

Despite this audacity, he was pardoned and returned to his house at Kilmorie, Skye.

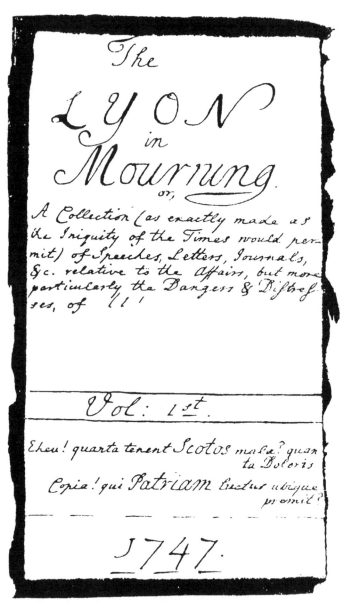

The
LYON
in
Mourning.
or,

A Collection (as exactly made as the Iniquity of the Times would permit) of Speeches, Letters, Journals, &c. relative to the Affairs, but more particularly the Dangers & Distresses, of

Vol: 1st.

Eheu! quarta tenent Scotos mala? quanta Doloris
Copia! qui Patriam lectus ubique premit?

1747.

Facsimile of original title page
(Courtesy of National Library of Scotland)

"THE LYON IN MOURNING"

by Revd. Kenneth Wigston

The Episcopal Church as such took no part in the Jacobite Risings but nearly everyone concerned was an Episcopalian, fighting for Scotland's Stewart Kings, for Scotland and the disbandment of the Union of 1707, and for the restoration of the Episcopal Church. The Jacobite army of 1715 were Episcopalian almost to a man, 70 per cent in the '45 were Episcopalian. Most Episcopalian clergy sympathised with the Jacobite Cause, either from principle or interest or both. Many gave it their open and active support. If they were not all Jacobite they were all punished for it and made to suffer, directly or indirectly, just the same.

One such person was the Rev. Robert Forbes, incumbent of Leith. In 1762 he became Bishop of Ross, Caithness and Argyll. He was born in 1708 and sent to Marischal College, Aberdeen, at the early age of fourteen, where he graduated M.A. in 1726. Ordained priest in 1735, he spent the rest of his life labouring and ministering at Leith, and, after he became Bishop, visiting his northern dioceses from time to time.

An ardent Jacobite, he set off in early September 1745 with others to join the Prince's Army but was arrested near Stirling and imprisoned in the Castle until February 1746 when he was moved to Edinburgh Castle. He was released in May 1746. He died at Leith on 18 November 1775.

From the stories of his fellow prisoners, and later other first-hand material, Bishop Forbes compiled his monumental "The Lyon in Mourning" in which he records the sufferings of the vanquished of Culloden. He accepted no account second hand and always sought corroboration from others. The collection was one of the good Bishop's most treasured possessions and he guarded it with the utmost jealousy. He could never be persuaded to publish because he thought it imprudent to print what would only be considered to be a censure on the Government of the day. "The Lyon in Mourning" was published in 1895 and reprinted in 1975.

Had it not been for his imprisonment, Bishop Forbes might have suffered a worse fate, along with the Rev. Robert Lyon, who, on 28 October 1746, although a non-combatant, was hung, drawn and quartered at Carlisle, and for no other reason than that he had served as a chaplain in the Prince's Army. Nor would there have been any "Lyon in Mourning" but for the single-mindedness of the good Bishop in collecting and recording these eye-witness accounts. Much of what is known of the 1745 Rising and its aftermath would never have come to light.

TIRNADRIS - PATTERN OF CHIVALRY

by Marion Cameron

(This is taken from a much longer article about Donald MacDonell of Tirnadris, the hero of the skirmish at Highbridge, on whom Sir Walter Scott modelled the Highland chief Fergus MacIvor in "Waverley". When researching for his novel, published in 1814, Scott had the inestimable advantage of being able to meet and interview some of the men who "Sixty Years Since" had taken part in the Rising.)

It was after the Battle of Falkirk (Friday 17 January '46) that sudden disaster struck him - "owing" he admitted freely, "to my own folly or rashness". That brief, "scrambling" engagement, fought towards early winter dusk in atrocious weather conditions of storm and "prodigious rain", though in the later stages fraught with confusion on both sides, had shown the numerically superior Government forces a poor match for Highlanders on their mettle, fighting at close range with their accustomed weapons. The Clan Donald Regiments had occupied their traditional place on the right of the Front Line and Jacobite losses had been light.

For some time after the battle the darkening scene remained confused, Plean Muir strewn with enemy dead, scattered remnants of General Hawley's troops still in flight from highland steel, the clansmen in disorderly chase.

Anxious that a total rout of Government forces be secured, Major MacDonell of Tirnadris urged on the pursuit. Chancing, in the dusk, upon a loitering group whom he took to be men from Lord John Drummond's (French) Royal Scots, or possibly General Stapleton's Irish Piquets, he strode towards them with characteristic impetuosity, demanding to know why they had broken off the pursuit. His startled dismay can only be imagined when the response came "by God - here's a rebel!" His own allegiance betrayed by the battle-soiled white cockade in his bonnet, he found himself seized by men from Barrel's Regiment and would have been shot out of hand. An intervention from Captain Lord Robert Kerr saved his life, but commanded surrender of his arms.

After this extraordinary mischance Tirnadris - the sole prisoner from the Prince's Army - was escorted by dragoons from Falkirk to Edinburgh Castle, and eventually to Carlisle.

In Carlisle Castle the prisoners of all ranks and circumstances were herded together like cattle in the Long Room of an inner ward (now long demolished) - intolerable conditions which Tirnadris dismissed drily as "much thronged". Later, even he admitted to having suffered briefly from "a little bit fever" but, being exceptionally robust, he recovered quickly.

The prison authorities were wary of the ingenuity and daring of men of the Tirnadris calibre; but, however strict the supervision, one concession allowed was leave to communicate by letter with relatives and friends and on 24 August Tirnadris wrote to the Rev. Robert Forbes: "They have not all got irons as yet; but they have not forgot me." In sending his compliments to Lady Bruce in Leith, he added: " . . . and to Mr Clark's family but especially to Miss Mally Clark and tell her that notwithstanding of my irons I could dance a Highland reel with her."

The light-hearted tone of the letter was clearly intended to hearten his anxious friends in Scotland - and doubtless also to camouflage his own dark thoughts. Arraignment was pending. Despite his naturally sanguine temperament, he must have been too well aware of the awful penalties still imposed under English Law upon men convicted of High Treason.

Yet his over-riding concern was not for himself but for the future welfare of "my poor wife". She would not, he assured her, be permitted to visit him in prison, and he urged strongly upon her to return home at once and attend to their affairs there. Presumably he had been kept in merciful ignorance that his home was already burned down and all the lands of Lochaber plundered and devastated.

His claim that a prison visit even from a spouse was forbidden may have been unfounded. But he "had not let her into the whole" and was determined to shield his cherished wife from the distress of seeing for herself the sordid circumstances to which a proud man had been reduced. But a far deeper feeling than pride was involved. In a letter to Robert Forbes he implored his support in keeping his wife from him, for "our parting would be more shocking to me than death".

As time passed and hope faded Tirnadris made what must have been a painful decision in requiring his only son, Ranald, to travel by chaise from Edinburgh to appear as a witness at his forthcoming trial. To expose a little boy of seven to such an ordeal seems uncharacteristic of Tirnadris. It is probable, therefore, that in his parlous situation he had been persuaded by his legal advisers that an innocent child, appearing in defence of his father's life, might arouse compassion and soften in some degree the damning weight of evidence against him.

Tirnadris was arraigned on 11 September and committed for trial. "I hope for the best," he wrote, "and prepare for the worst." He refused to plead guilty. There appears to be no record of testimony given by Ranald or even if he was present during these grim proceedings. All that is known is that the child was living at Warwick Hall near Carlisle at that time.

Alexander Lockhart, advocate for the defence, was appalled by the savage penalties for treason still imposed by English law and deeply impressed by and concerned for his client. Emotionally involved, therefore, to a conspicuous degree, he did his utmost "most handsomely" for the accused man. "Really", wrote Tirnadris when all was over, "there never came a more eloquent discourse", and "my good and worthy friend Mr Lockhart would tear them all to pieces if justice or law was regarded." But the case was hopeless. The jury "made no doubt" that Tirnadris was guilty of High Treason, and Judge Denison pronounced the dreadful sentence accordingly.

Now the last frail hope was gone. Throughout the dark weeks of waiting which ensued, while the Jacobite prisoners were depleted by removal for execution, Tirnadris retained that "cheerfulness of temper with which he bore up under all his sufferings." Profoundly convinced of the justice of his cause, he at no time felt any regret for his part in the Rising, only a calm resolve, as he said, "to goe to death as a Christian and a man of honour ought."

On Saturday the 18 October, the day appointed for his death, Donald MacDonell of Tirnadris, with Kinlochmoidart and seven other condemned men, were drawn by sledge from the Castle to the place of execution on Harraby Hill about a mile distant on the road between Carlisle and Penrith. On that market day the assembled crowds saw in Tirnadris a man rendered sallow, haggard but still unbroken after eight consecutive months of harsh confinement and, as a last indignity, refused permission to deliver his dying speech.

Sir Walter Scott's description of "Fergus's" last journey may well have derived from eye-witness accounts: a black-painted sledge bearing the executioner with the condemned and drawn by white horses, the military escort slow-marching to a dirge of funeral music and the tolling of a muffled bell - theatrical effects surveyed by Tirnadris with ironic contempt, yet, as ever, with courage and dignity.

When in something under two hours, the soldiers marched briskly back to the Castle the fifes and kettledrums now played a sprightly tune, intimating that yet another batch of "traitors" had been duly extirpated.

And, when, indeed, having committed his soul to "Divine and allwise providence" Major MacDonell stood bound and noosed on the scaffold it seemed certain that within the next cruel hour the story of Tirnadris must finally end and, in time, all memory of him fade.

Yet destiny decreed otherwise. Thanks to the fidelity of his friends, to the scrupulous records of Bishop Forbes and to the genius of a man he never knew, the figure of Tirnadris will live on through generations to come - archetypal Highland gentleman, epitome of gallantry and chivalry.

THE ADVENTURES OF RANALD

by Marion Cameron

Some three years after his father's death, Ranald left in Cumberland a quaint record entitled "The Adventures of Ranald MacDonell from seven years of age till his arrival at Warwick Hall. Written by himself, 1749." From the pen of a child of ten, writing in a recently learned language from the recollections of three years earlier, this is a remarkable document. Although acknowledging ever-present danger, it is innocent of any trace of bravado or exaggeration, in tone ingenuous and unselfconscious, like a child talking aloud. The figure which emerges is that of a plucky, high-spirited little boy with unusual powers of perception and recall.

His record begins at the time when punitive bands of Hanoverian soldiery, ravaging the Highlands, were closing in upon Brae Lochaber: "After the Battle of Culloden the cruelty of the soldiers made us fly from our houses . . ." Warned in time, the family at Tirnadris House hurriedly loaded their horses with what was readily portable of clothing, provisions and bedding and, driving their livestock before them, followed on foot for two miles to a sequestered glen "beside a little water that was at the bottom of two hills." Early next morning they moved on to Loch Treig, hoping to find there a trusted friend, Ronald Angus. This clansman, however, was still absent from home and feared killed at Culloden. Mrs. MacDonall of Tirnadris, accompanied by her small stepson, then sought out her sister across the loch, but this lady proved to be laid low with smallpox.

Soon afterwards a crippling back pain signified that the little boy had been infected. Carried by a maidservant, he was put to bed ". . . I was very bad of the smallpox . . . I was blind for about a week . . . then I got up and was very well. Then we went to Ranach to get further from the soldiers whom we heard were near hand us. My stepmother, the gentleman, my eldest sister and me went to Ranach through woods and over mountains on foot . . . and the gentleman used to roll me in his plaid with himself and sometimes we walked all night when we heard the soldiers were near us."

At this time of great danger they encountered Keppoch's son and entire family making their escape, ". . . but we had little time to stay with them, for we heard the Soldiers were coming."

After a hurried parting from their kinsfolk they continued their flight on foot throughout the following night and until seven o'clock next evening; then, hiding in a glen, the exhausted party "had four miles to go for wood . . . and as far for water." After three days in a rough shelter there, they were found by Ronald Angus - returned safely, after all, from Culloden - with his brother Samuel and another man.

In recording their desperate game of hide and seek with the ruthless redcoats, Ranald tells his story with verve and spirit, doing his best to keep track of location and time. Guided and protected now by the two loyal brothers, the fugitives set out at six o'clock next morning, ". . . and they gave me a little galloway and they went themselves on foot, and they ran all the way as the galloway trotted; and about eight o'clock we got to our journey's end." But here again they encountered imminent danger, for "We saw a drove of cattle and some gentlemen that had been along with the Prince flying from their houses."

After two further days in the heather, they concealed themselves in a wood, subsisting on milk, crowdie cheese and fish. "There was a loch near the wood, and Samuel Angus used to fish and struck fire with his flint to make a fire to broil them." Then, having intelligence that the coast was clear, they made a laborious trek back towards Loch Treig, drove their cattle across a river and remained in an improvised shelter for about a fortnight. A few days of watching from a nearby wood seemed to indicate that it was now safe to return to Ronald Angus's house, where they remained for a further fortnight. At this time young Ranald had a near escape from death. Driving the cattle back from grazing on an island in mid-river, he found himself out of his depth. ". . . the water was so deep it came into my mouth, and I stumbled in the middle of it and had like to have been drowned, but Samuel Angus came and saved me."

On learning that Brae Lochaber was now clear of the redcoats, Ranald's stepmother ventured a return to Spean Bridge - only to find that Tirnadris House had been burned down. For a time the family sheltered in "a little house of wood and turfs. A little after I heard that I was to go to a gentleman's house in England, and two gentlemen had come to meet me. In the afternoon my Uncle and a lad that could talk English and us, we all went to Ronald Angus's house." They started for Rannoch next morning, escorted over the first twelve miles by the two faithful brothers, ". . . then Ronald Angus and Samuel and the other man took their leave of me . . ."

From this point onwards Ranald's narrative becomes vague as to time and place, with an underlying sense of mystery and perplexity. "That lad who could talk English went along with me till I came to Edinburgh, and I got English clothes and I did not love myself in them." Obviously bewildered in the streets of the city, Ranald, in the care of the officious Mrs. Douglas, was hustled to a variety of houses and presented to a succession of strangers." I went one day to see a lady and she gave me a guinea." Later, Mrs Douglas demanded to see the coin, "but she put it in her purse and I never saw more on't."

After the confusions of his stay in Edinburgh, Ranald chose to cover the sequel in a few brief sentences." Then Mrs. Douglas and I set out for Carlisle in a chaise and we dined with some French officers at Carlisle and then we went back to Edinburgh."

(Ranald makes no other reference to Carlisle or what happened there).

Before, during and for some time after the trial and death of Major Donald MacDonell of Tirnadris, his widow and young daughters lived as guests of Francis and Jane Warwick at Warwick Hall, four miles east of Carlisle. From this kindly refuge they dispersed gradually and, as the family chronicler observed, "the children of suffering became blessings and ornaments of society."

(Ranald spent some eight months at Traquair before returning to Warwick Hall).

Travellers approaching Carlisle from the North would pass through the Scotch Gate. And there still, and for many years to come, were conspicuously impaled the severed heads of Tirnadris and Kinlochmoidart. Ranald said only, "... next morning we came to Warwick, where I was kindly received." And thus he concluded the story of his "Adventures".

The warmth of Ranald's welcome to Warwick Hall must have been comforting, as was the tranquility of the mellowed mansion house which with its policies had stood for many centuries on the banks of the River Eden nearby an old four-arched bridge.

Politically uncommitted as was Francis Warwick himself, his wife Jane - a sister of Howard of Greystock, later Duke of Norfolk - was enthusiastically Jacobite in sentiment. In November of the previous year she had entertained the Prince to dinner and called down blessings on his head. Now, despite the "stern disapprobation" of the authorities, it must have given her delight to take the son of an executed Jacobite to her heart. However distressing had been the circumstances of Ranald's earlier stay at Warwick Hall, the couple apparently had become devoted to him; for now, they themselves being childless, they announced their decision to adopt him as their own son - and thus presumably heir to high social status, wealth and property.

There is no detailed record of the ten years or so passed by Ranald at Warwick Hall. No doubt his kindly adoptive parents counted themselves fortunate in having appointed this clever, personable "young man of great promise" as the Warwick heir, in due time to make a suitable marriage and so carry on into the future, even if not in direct line, their ancient name and heritage.

It is doubtful, however, if the prospect of adorning the squirearchy made any appeal to Ranald himself. A Gael to the marrow of his bones, he had detested the wearing of fashionable "English clothes" and, as his narrative disclosed, longed for the sound of his native tongue. A courteous boy, always ready to acknowledge a kindness, he doubtless kept his thoughts to himself. He was of a studious disposition, and his indulgent adoptive parents gave him every facility to pursue his studies: "No expense or pains were spared in his education."

Because of the boy's air of reserve, it was decided by Mr. and Mrs. Warwick that a period abroad to complete his studies would be salutary; and the Seminary chosen was the Scots College at Douai - then and until the Revolution situated in northern France. When he had reached the age of about eighteen Ranald intimated from Douai that his wish was to continue his studies there with a view to ordination to the priesthood - news which was received with dismay.

The reaction of his eldest sister Isabella - who had shared his Highland memories and adventures - is recorded. Isabella, outraged by this news, "strongly objected" to her brother's decision. In her opinion it would always remain Ranald's clear duty to hold himself in readiness to obey their father's last command - to fight in the Stuart cause if, and when, any occasion should offer. And she left her brother in no doubt of her anger. In reply to her remonstrances, the family chronicler refers to two letters from Douai, dated respectively 13 and 30 June 1757, which, though unquoted, are described as "affectionate, temperate, but firm" - qualities which seem to summarise the character of the young writer himself. Clearly, the youth's sense of vocation was powerful.

The private path which had led Ranald to this point remains, like so much else, known only to himself. All that is recorded further is that his longing for ordination was never fulfilled. When he was in about his twentieth year, news reached his family from France that Ranald had died at Douai.

"LOYALTY UNLEARNED; HONOUR UNTAUGHT"
(Shakespeare)

by Joan Young

The Gentleman's Magazine for May 1753 records that "Dr. Archibald Cameron was brought from the Tower under a strong guard to the King's Bench, Westminster, and there arraigned upon the Act of Attainder passed against him and others for being concerned in the late rebellion, and not surrendering in due time."

The son of John Cameron (18th of Lochiel) and brother of the Gentle Lochiel, Archibald Cameron studied medicine in Glasgow, Edinburgh and Paris. He then settled down in his native Lochaber, devoting himself to the welfare of his fellow clansmen.

A gentle, civilised man, he probably had little enthusiasm for the campaign of 1745; not through lack of loyalty to the Stuart cause, but because he shared his brother's fears that, without substantial French aid, it was doomed and would bring only disaster to Scotland.

In fact, Lochiel sent his brother, Archie, to urge the Prince to return home. But Charles had already given his answer to the same advice tendered by other Highland chiefs: "I am come home." What Highlander could resist such an appeal to his chivalry?

So Lochiel brought out his clan and, "Upon this", says an eye-witness, "depended the whole undertaking." Archie Cameron was appointed physician, with the rank of Captain, in the Jacobite army. He was present at Prestonpans, Falkirk, where he was wounded, and at the final tragedy of Culloden. He used his medical skill for the benefit of friend and foe alike.

When, after Culloden, the Prince took to the heather, Archie Cameron remained in contact with him. He joined him in Cluny's famous "Cage" on Ben Alder, and brought news of the arrival of two French ships at Loch nan Uamh. He was with the royal party when it finally sailed for France.

Devoted to Lochiel, the Prince was instrumental in securing his appointment as Colonel of Albany's Regiment. It was an appointment accepted very reluctantly by the Cameron chief, whose one thought was another rising. Only that could save "the people I have undone", he wrote passionately to King James.

In 1753 Archie Cameron was in Scotland in connection with the money the Prince had left with Cluny - and to sound out feeling. He was betrayed by Pickle the Spy, and arrested at Stewart of Glenbuckie's by soldiers from the garrison at Inversnaid.

Lodged in Edinburgh Castle, he was later taken to London and the Tower. Probably to conceal the identity of Pickle, Archie Cameron was sentenced to death on the seven year old Attainder. He was to die in the revolting manner dreamed up by Edward I, as the penalty for treason and then still in force.

On June 7th, dressed in a light coat, red waistcoat and breeches and a new bag wig, Archie Cameron was executed at Tyburn. On the same day George II drove to Parliament, and among the Acts to which he gave the royal assent was one to "continue the disarming of the Highlands."

Commenting on Archie Cameron's death, the Scots Magazine 1753 writes, "His merit is confessed by all parties and his death can hardly be called untimely as his behaviour rendered his last day worth an age of common life."

He was buried in the Savoy Chapel where, years later, a monument was raised to his memory by his great-grandson Charles Hay Cameron. This was destroyed in the chapel fire of 1864 and later replaced by a stained glass window designed by Burne-Jones.

Archie Cameron and his brother Lochiel, who died in exile without seeing Scotland again, represented all that was best in Highland culture and tradition. It was undoubtedly to save that culture, as well as to serve their Prince, that many Highlanders came "out" in 1745.

The Badge of Clan Cameron

IN REMEMBRANCE OF DR. ARCHIBALD CAMERON

by Victoria Thorpe

On 7 June 1993, some seventy people gathered at the Queen's Chapel of the Savoy in order to honour the memory of the last Jacobite martyr. The occasion marked the 240th anniversary of Dr. Archibald Cameron's execution at Tyburn in 1753 and was prompted by the need to replace a memorial already twice lost over the last hundred years.

By courtesy of the Duchy of Lancaster, who administer the Chapel, a beautiful brass plaque has now been inset into the altar plinth.

It was upon the instigation of the present Lochiel that the matter of the missing plaque was first taken up by the 1745 Association and the presence of Sir Donald along with many of his family and other descendants of Dr. Archibald Cameron provided a fitting tribute to the brave Jacobite. The 1745 Association and The Royal Stuart Society were well represented and the attendance of the present Chief of Clan MacPherson recalled Dr. Archie's close links with Cluny MacPherson of the 'Forty-Five and the Loch Arkaig gold. Wreaths were laid to the accompaniment of the lament 'Lochaber No More', played by Pipe Major Brian MacRae, Piper to Her Majesty the Queen.

In the Bidding, the Reverend John Robson, Chaplain of the Royal Victorian Order, who conducted the service, said . . .

Dr. Cameron was universally loved and respected, not only amongst his own clansmen, but amongst friend and foe alike for he was of 'so humane a Disposition that when wounded Prisoners were brought to him, he was as assiduous in his care of them, as if they had fought in the cause he espoused.'

In his last message from the Tower, written 'with a poor blunted pencil that had escaped the diligence of my searchers,' Dr. Cameron stated his adherence to the Scottish Episcopal Church and his loyalty to the exiled Stuarts. Of Prince Charles Edward Stuart he had nothing but praise, declaring that he 'became more and more captivated with his amiable and princely virtues which are indeed in every instance so eminently great as I want words to describe.' He continued, 'I can further affirm (and my present situation and that of my dear Prince can leave no room to suspect me of flattery) that as I have been his companion in the lowest degree of adversity ever prince was reduced to, so I have beheld him too on the highest pinnacle of glory. Yet he was always the same, ever affable and courteous, giving constant proofs of his great humanity and of his love for his friends and country."

Dr. Cameron met his death with courage and resolution, proudly denying the charges brought against him by an unjust government and declaring that 'neither the fear of the worst death their malice could invent nor much less their flattering promises' could have led him into betraying his friends.

In a final letter to his son in France he wrote, 'I am far less concerned about myself than about my Friends and ruined Country: They, not I, claim Pity, tho' I fall victim to Truth, Honour and Uprightness, by the Rage of Hanovarian Councils, the declared Enemies to every Virtue . . . I should rather sacrifice my Life than save it on dishonourable Terms. I thank my God, I was always easier Ashamed than Frightened.'

David Lumsden of Cushnie, President of the 1745 Association, whose own ancestors fought for the Stuarts, gave a magnificent address, part of which is included here . . .

The memorial dedicated today is the third. The first was a tablet erected by Dr. Archibald Cameron's grandson, Charles Hay Cameron in 1846 and destroyed by fire in 1864. The second, a beautiful stained glass window by Sir Edward Burne-Jones, was destroyed during the bombing of the Second World War. This window had been erected in 1870 by Charles Lloyd Norman. He had married into the Cameron family and his wife was a direct descendant of Dr. Archibald's third son known as Donald the Banker. A number of his descendants, including his great grand-daughter, are present at this service. All are descended from Charles Hay Cameron who erected the first memorial tablet for his grandfather.

I am honoured to be asked to give this Address. As you know, we Scots revere, almost worship our ancestors. I was brought up with the knowledge of the exploits of my small but ancient family, and the Risings of 1715 and 1745. Two of us fought at Culloden: young Cushnie was killed but Andrew, the Prince's secretary, after four months skulking in the Highlands, escaped to Edinburgh as the liveried groom of a Lady, riding behind him paddle style in the fashion of the time, his yellow locks replaced by a black wig and eyebrows corked. He reached London disguised as a poor teacher in rusty black garments - in his pocket a tiny Virgil and Horace, badges of his profession and companions on a weary fortnight's ride. Thus disguised, he visited his friends and associates in Newgate Prison. For such audacity, his father, William, who had been out in the '15, said he deserved to be hanged. After escaping to France he applied for a commission in the regiment Lochiel had got from the King of France. Shortly afterwards he rejoined the Prince and King James appointed him *his* secretary. His correspondence at the exiled court was voluminous but he found the time to write his magnum opus on the Antiquities of Rome. Andrew's name is always linked with that of his sister, Isabella, wife of his friend of the '45, the engraver, Sir Robert Strange. The memoirs of Sir Robert Strange and Andrew Lumsden make delightful reading and paint a vivid picture of the time, particularly of life at the Jacobite court.

Although not a native speaker, I would like to end by quoting a few lines from the 'Oran do'n Phrionnsa' that great Gaelic battle hymn of welcome to the Prince, written by Alasdair MacMhaighstir Alasdair, Bard to Clan Ranald, in Moidart on the eve of the '45, lines that would have inspired Dr. Archibald *then* as they do us today.

'S aoibhinn leam-sa, tha e tighinn
Mac an Righ dlighich tha bhuainn
Slíos mòr righeal d'an tig aramachd
Claidheamh 'is targaid nan dual

Torman do phíoba 'is do bhràtaich
Chuireadh 'ad spíorad bràs 'san t-sluagh
Dh'eireadh ar n-àrden 'is ar n-àigne
'S cuireamaid air a phrasgan ruaig.

Joyous to me his coming, son of the rightful King. A great royal figure to whom an army will come, sword and targe at the ready. The rumble of the pipes and the banner would put a bold spirit into the force, raise our mood and vigour. Let us put the enemy rabble to flight.

The unicorn emblem of the House of Stuart

97

THE 1745 ASSOCIATION

Patrons

The Earl of Perth
Lord Ogilvy
The Earl of Airlie
Sir Donald Cameron of Lochiel, K.T., C.V.O.

Office Bearers

President:
Baron David Lumsden of Cushnie, M.A. (Cantab), F.S.A. (Scot)
Garioch Pursuivant of Arms

Chairman:
Norman H. MacDonald, F.R.S.A, F.S.A. (Scot)

Vice-Chairmen:
Mrs. Betty Stuart Hart, M.A. (Cantab)
Miss. K. Anne Scholey, B.A. Hons. (London)
Mr. F. Peter Lole

Hon. Secretary:
Miss Christian W.H. Aikman
Ferry Cottage, Corran, Ardgour, Fort William, Inverness-shire PH33 7AA
Telephone: (0855) 841306

Hon. Treasurer:
Revd. Kenneth Wigston

Editor of "The Jacobite":
Mrs. B.S. Hart

*If you would like to know more about the 1745 Association,
please contact our Secretary, Miss Christian Aikman.*